OPULENCE

OPULENCE

MASTERING YOUR FINANCES, POWER, AND MINDSET

RAHGOR

Madison **+** Park

A Global Branding Agency

This book is dedicated to
Debbie McRae & Lisa Arrington

Throughout my journey of studying and creating wealth, I've come across various public figures that have shared their knowledge on aspects of building wealth. Although some have been viewed as controversial, I still value the truth that they have shared on the subject of wealth. It is in my heart and vision that each reader that lays their eyes on these pages gain something from my notes to help them accumulate wealth in whatever form that may be in their eyes.

This book will be updated continuously over the years with the intent to be used as another tool for all those who seek to attain a wealth of balance and abundance.

"Capital goes where it's welcome and stays where it's well treated."

—Walter Wriston (former chairman and CEO of Citicorp)

Contents

Contents

Contents

The Opulence Manifesto

T his declaration is for the individual who has the potential to be financially and spiritually wealthy, at the highest capacity that they can sustain, but has challenges in realizing the goal. Such challenges may be the result of having a **"Premature Mindset."**

Premature means "occurring or done before the usual or proper time." In other words, it means being "too early." If you're in a premature mindset, you may have a financial goal to reach seven-figures, or build something impressive in this world that will allow you to be spiritually aligned, but achieving that goal could be stalled by any of the following:

- You are thinking on a low level.
- You are interacting with the wrong group of individuals.
- Your environment might not cultivate the energy and space you need to develop your skill/talent.
- Your belief system might be weak.
- Your work ethic isn't effective enough to produce great results.

This does not mean that you don't have the potential to be wealthy, a dynamic business leader, or a global servant to humanity. It just means that you are getting ahead of yourself in making your goal a reality. Before it can manifest, you need to change your mindset and personal belief system to make the internal and external shifts that are necessary to help you achieve results at a higher capacity.

Freedom is the end goal. Having freedom allows you to spend more of your God-given time developing yourself and finding solutions to problems within your personal life, local community, country, and world. This manifesto is a full commitment and declaration that you will think, plan, work, pray, grow, move, and achieve breakthroughs on a supreme level. At this very moment, you will let go of the old patterns you once followed and begin creating new patterns that will have you operating at optimal performance.

As you begin to declare this over your life, remember to appreciate every opportunity and every monetary blessing that comes your way.

The Opulence Declaration

I, _____, will give my entire life to the vision of becoming wealthy financially and spiritually. I will move forward with great clarity in my vision and daily actions. I will be radical in thinking, intense in action, and highly driven to attain unimaginable results. Today, I will only entertain the subject matter that pertains to the changes and elevation I want to see and be.

I, _____, vow to embrace all moments that call for me to be a blueprint to someone else. I accept all challenges and hardships that come with this new life of mine. I also accept and fully engage in the celebration of all that is to come once I achieve my goal of becoming financially and spiritually wealthy from the new habits I have mastered.

I, _____, will protect and serve the individuals and communities that support me as I move from having lack of to more than enough, due to my achieved goal(s). I will not sit by and watch any of these individuals or communities suffer due to selfish acts by others. I vow to be a resource, inspiration, and problem-solver for them in whatever capacity God makes able.

I PROMISE TO . . .

1. Meditate at least fifteen minutes a day and talk with God, continuously, for clarity.

2. Establish a diverse and wise circle of advisors and elders.

3. Make sure I have gathered all facts, executed solid research, and consulted with my circle of advisors before I make any major decisions.

4. Attain the best and most valuable information that can put me in the best position in my personal and business life.

5. Make my presence felt in the communities that support me through various philanthropic projects and donations.

6. Never sacrifice healthy and positive relationships, of any kind, for selfish gain.

7. Master my emotions so that I can think clearly to make the best decisions.

8. Serve in the highest form of my ability.

9. Be the lender and not the slave.

10. Fact check all information given to me by others. If the source isn't credible, I will not adhere to it.

11. Never make important life decisions based upon personal opinions.

12. Have complete clarity prior to any agreement I make in my business and personal life.

13. Engage in great preparation and partnerships to achieve my goals.

14. Value my time and the time of others.

15. Indulge in the learning process to know more so that I can do more.

16. Remember that progress is perfection.

17. Test the full capacity of my faith and lean on the favor that God has given me.

18. Fear no noun (person, place, or thing).

19. Be relentless in my discipline, dedication, and determination to achieve my goal.

20. Maximize all my current and forthcoming resources.

21. Create all things with a focus on detail and high quality.

22. Have an immaculate work ethic.

23. Challenge myself to enjoy life to the maximum.

24. Establish and master an effective financial management and investment system.

25. Never doubt my genius or ability to achieve the vision that I have set forth for myself.

I, _____, promise to do and be all these things with unwavering faith. As I begin this new way of moving from potential to actual, I will allow the universe to constantly remind me that my location is not my destination.

_____

PRINT FULL NAME

_____

SIGNATURE

_____

DATE

Introduction

I lost it. I lost it all in a matter of months. A few years ago, I experienced one of my lowest moments, one that was accompanied by incredible pain and disappointment within myself. Despite all that I had accomplished and all that I stood for, I made some life-changing mistakes with my relationships, finances, self-love, and inner peace. I've had some hardships in my life as a young person, but as a man, and becoming a strong man, I really felt this one.

During this moment, I remember calling my grandmother and telling her that I had damn near lost everything. I'd been staying with extended family for a while, but it was time that I found a permanent place so that I could get back on my feet. I was looking everywhere for a place to stay prior to calling her, and my time to make a decision was running out. Right then, I thought I only had two options—I would either stay at my grandparents or my spiritual mother's home. I was almost at wits' end. I didn't know where to go or what to do. The thought of a shelter started to dance in my mind, but every single day I battled that thought, because I'd experienced that environment as a young person and I was committed to never allowing myself to get to that point, no matter what.

When I started talking to my grandmother, my eyes were beginning to water. I was embarrassed and so disappointed in myself. I was mad that I'd never given myself the opportunity to grow in a way that might have prevented this situation. I hesitated a bit in our conversation, engaging in random small talk. Finally, I slowly explained the situation and asked her if I could stay at the house for just a short period of time until I got myself together. I really didn't want to ask or be there, but I felt that it was the best decision to make at that time. My grandmother didn't make it easy—she asked me so many questions, but I just needed a place to stay.

Despite all our discussion, she couldn't give me a straight answer, because she had to talk it over with my grandfather. So we hung up the phone, and I waited outside of the house that I was staying at until she called me back. When I saw her name pop up on my phone, I knew it would be a definite yes, but I was totally wrong. My grandmother was in tears and sobbing over the phone as she told me that my grandfather had said no, I could not stay. My heart dropped so low, and I began to cry. I felt like my eyes have been in tears for months with all that I was dealing with and carrying burdens that no one around me knew about.

I had begun accepting full responsibility for my actions that had led me to this moment, but I still couldn't see the light at the end of the tunnel. When things started to feel like the walls were closing in, I "knew" my grandparents would come through, so I wasn't at all ready for her statement. When I realized I couldn't depend on my grandparents to help me through this, I felt so much hurt and shock at the same time.

Wait . . . I am your grandson; you know where I'm trying to go, you know the pressure I was dealing with due to the work I was involved in, you know my heart has always been in the right place. Why are you going to let me suffer like this? You're going to let me struggle out here and embarrass myself like this? I became quiet over the phone after hearing her answer, but I was losing it on the inside. All I could do was accept what was happening all around me and within me. I drew a blank and just surrendered—I was completely done.

As if from a long distance, I heard her heartbroken voice saying, "I'm sorry baby, but I can't help you, and your grandfather said no as well. Let this be a lesson for you as you continue to go through this phase of your life as a man. God will take care of you, and you must believe that he will. God never gives you more than you can bear. You will be fine. Have faith." My grandmother's voice was as gentle as a dove, but as strong as God's power in our weakest moments. Her wise words hit my spirit, but that didn't stop the flood of sorrow I was feeling for my current life. She went on to say, "I love you," and then the phone hung up.

After that, I just remember hearing a voice in my head saying that their home was no longer my home. All those years, it had been. My grandparents would say, "You can always come back home when you hit your low point and need to get back on your feet." But that was no longer true. I had to realize that it was no longer home for me; I had to become a balanced man and cultivate the energy to find my place under the sun on this planet, to create an environment I could truly call my home. They hadn't put me in this situation, I had. They didn't have authority or responsibility over me, I do.

That's real power—the power of understanding. There is power in recognizing that your mindset will sometimes allow you to accept years of dwelling in an environment that makes you feel like you don't hold the key to unlocking a new way of living, a new expression of life, or a new way of walking in the abundance of your power to be truly of wealth.

I stood there outside, saying to myself, "I have no home. I have no safety net." Then I remembered the performance coach, Tony Robbins, and his talk about affirmations and incantations. I just stood tall, smirked, and said with full authority to God, "Never again, God. Never again will I allow myself to be in this situation, ever again. I *am* dynamic, great, wealthy, powerful, and worthy."

What good is a man whose foundation is weak? What good is he as a husband, partner, friend, or business partner if he is not whole at his own core? I believe that my grandfather's underlying purpose of telling me no, through my grandmother, was to make sure I strengthened my foundation, and became whole at my core. He wouldn't accept anything less of his grandson than being a strong and powerful man in this lifetime. Yes, my waters were rough, but I needed to steer my own ship through them, because calm waters never made a strong sailor.

I revisited the idea of reaching out to my spiritual mother, who lived close to my grandparents. When I did, I told her what had happened, what was going on in my life. I was very hesitant, because I never wanted to be or feel like a burden to others, so it was very hard to ask for help. After hearing "no" so much, I was nervous that this would be her answer, but, she said "yes" and welcomed me with open arms.

I stayed in her basement for what was supposed to be a few weeks but ended up being close to six or seven months. She made it as warm and welcoming as she possibly could for me. I battled so many internal thoughts and emotions during that time, because staying in the basement brought me back to those days with my father and brother and all that we'd been through (I won't get into too much detail with that here— you'll have to read my memoir, *ONE23*, to get a full understanding). The air mattress in that basement became my bed of comfort and a reminder that I was about to go through a transformation like I never had before. I just started giving thanks for this woman in my life who stepped in and every single day poured into me her presence, love, and understanding, even when I knew that my need was an unexpected surprise.

During that time, each and every day, I started working on myself. I needed strength, stability, and higher self-standards. All that I was going through was because I'd made poor decisions for my own life, and I had to take responsibility for that as a man. I started fasting and praying, asking God to show me a way up and out, to show me where I needed to be and what tools and knowledge I needed. For years, I would read proverbs daily and study everything I could about wealth creation.

Soon, inspired by my studies, I made an unwavering commitment to be the embodiment of wealth creation in various forms. I knew that I had to be emotionally and physiologically stable to make sound decisions over my life. But this was also true for building wealth. I made a commitment to move on from the mindset of relying on someone else to be my safety net, to make someone else's space my dwelling. You must understand that I felt powerless at times, lacking fullness. I wasn't expressing myself in the most authentic and comfortable way—I couldn't do that in the places I crashed for long periods of time, because they weren't my space, weren't of my authentic choosing. I was only there because I'd made past decisions that had forced me to humble myself and accept whatever was accessible to me. Life can do that to us sometimes, but if it's self-inflicted, the only way to change it is to change yourself.

Over time, I started to make progress and leverage the knowledge and ancient wisdom that was either bestowed upon me or that I found through my research and studies. I made progress, though of course I stumbled here and there, making some sound decisions and some not-so-good decisions throughout the process. But I was well on my way. Fast forward a few years later, and here I am, sharing with you the insight and lessons I learned from some of the most brilliant minds that came across my path in one form or another. Today, I'm standing stronger, more aware of myself, and continuing on the path of wealth creation so that I can be a resource and teacher to those who want to build wealth from the inside first, so they won't get too caught up in the wealth they will attract and see surrounding them on the outside.

My spiritual mother said to me toward the end of my stay with her, **"Watch the tables you place your feet under."** It was the perfect jewel to put on my crown before I stepped back on the road that was now set before me. I was now in a better position to plant new seeds; to harvest, cook, and buy food. Because of this, I would be invited to many tables, in many different environments. Some would be of good cheer, while others might be the reason I shed a tear. So because of this, I should always be aware of who I am, where I am, and how I got here. My presence is beautiful, and I have to be aware of where I place myself and the food I now have.

Her words ring loud to me every day as a reminder that I've been through too much at this point to dim my light with whom I sit with and eat with, or the invitations I accept in life.

This is a book for you to use in many ways. It contains insights about what I've learned, studied, and mastered for the elevation of myself. This book dives into the notes I created for myself as a guide to creating wealth internally and financially. I pray that this book is a miracle to many and is pointless to none. May every eye that sees these words and every hand that touches this book be changed, moved, and inspired to create wealth and live abundantly.

Becoming the man I've always yearned to be is still a journey in progress. I'm still walking on the path of wealth creation. The knowledge I have been given and will share here is always being refined, enhanced, and applied. So just know that if you accept and commit to this path, we are walking it together.

MASTER YOUR FINANCES.
MASTER YOUR POWER.
MASTER YOUR MINDSET.

AND SOON, YOU WILL
SEE AND KNOW
WHAT OPULENCE
IS ALL ABOUT.

LET ME GUIDE AND
COACH YOU THROUGH IT.

LOVE + LIGHT

〜

RAHGOR

I felt uneasy believing
I couldn't be wealthy because
of my skin color or because
I wasn't from a particular
area. So, I decided to destroy
that mindset . . .

Opulence

1

What Is Opulence?

W hen I decided on writing this book, I was wondering if all my readers from around the world would be familiar with the word "opulence." It's a term that has been used worldwide many times but has been associated with only a small group of individuals. When the word comes to mind, I know that I'm looking at something or someone who embodies something in its highest form.

Opulence, by definition, means great wealth or luxuriousness. Those who are considered opulent have a great deal of wealth or affluence. They are abundant in more ways than one. A little history about the word is that it's borrowed from Middle French and Latin—*opulentia*, from *opulentus*, meaning "abounding in resources." Those who are opulent are considered to be exhibiting or characterized by opulence.

Being that opulence involves the word "wealth," I believe it's important to make sure you are clear on this term as well. Wealth, by definition, means an abundance of valuable possessions or money—the state of being rich; material prosperity; abundant supply. But there is also another side to the definition of wealth. The term is also defined by the ability to experience life in its full capacity. This can be in the form of family, friendships, the ability to eat every single day, or access to help another person experience the freedom you have of enjoying life in its full capacity.

Wealth is cultivated and attracted by those who are willing to create space for it. The ones who establish their mindset so that when wealth is all around them, they are able to sustain it so that it can be enjoyed by future generations to come. This is just a piece of understanding wealth and how it ties into the lifestyle of opulence.

Understanding Opulence

We must understand that the universe and all that is within it is opulence. All that we create comes from the universe. From our thoughts, to the words we speak, to the material we use—all comes from the universe. Every human being has a great deal of wealth within themselves.

The Purpose and Reason for This Book

The reason I decided to write this book is because I wanted to share the knowledge, experience, and wisdom that helped me with my shortcomings in my business and personal life. I didn't come from a wealthy family, nor did I seem to have the right information about building true wealth in all its forms. At some point in my life, I decided to stop blaming my parents and others for not sharing with me the insight I needed in order to get out of poverty.

When I would hang out with some of my friends, I grew tired of hearing about what group of people had all the wealth and how it wasn't in our cards to have that type of wealth. I felt different about that. I felt uneasy believing I couldn't be wealthy because of my skin color or because I wasn't from a particular area. So, I decided to destroy that mindset, to stay far away from it. After all, I was tired of coming up short and being surrounded in poverty-stricken environments.

I wanted freedom, and I knew that if I was to attain it, attain true freedom, I needed to begin where I was and take full responsibility for myself. If I chose to, I could read, write, and work my ass off to attain what seemed like a dream to many—but not to me. My desire was to serve others around the world at my highest capacity, not having to worry about any type of debt hanging over my head. I wanted to walk, talk, and think on another level.

And that's exactly what I did. For the past seven years, I've committed to enhancing my financial IQ. I decided to take the leap of faith by embarking on a journey toward financial freedom and getting a full understanding of how to build true and great wealth.

As an entrepreneur, I had many great ideas, but I couldn't get them funded. I watched people who praised me for my previous and current work, but declined my business proposals just to give business to someone who couldn't do half of what I was capable of doing. I told myself I would never again sweat and waste my time looking for someone to believe in me. In light of this, I put fire under my seat so that I could have more than enough to fund my own ideas, projects, and dreams.

What I wanted was freedom in all of its facets. And I vowed that I would be a living example of opulence, a person of great wealth financially, and also in wisdom, experiences, and energy. I wanted to make sure I was able to teach along the journey. I wanted to make sure that all those who followed me, young and old, would receive truth about what it takes to attain wealth—the sacrifices, the emotional rollercoaster, the pitfalls, the time consumption, the heartaches, the little moments, the big moments, the missed opportunities, the transformation, the setbacks, the leaps, the extraordinary discipline, and the unwavering faith one must have to achieve tremendous goals.

If you are in financial or spiritual bondage, or both, this book is for you. If you are a single parent trying to make ends meet, this book is for you. If you are an executive of a company, or if you are a new graduate fresh out of school with a new position, this book is for you. If you are a person in a homeless shelter because of unforeseen circumstances, this book is for you. No matter your background, color, religion, or economic status, this book is a guide to help you along the way to achieving freedom. I created this book knowing that I was able to reach a status of wealth because of the information I sought, the wisdom that was passed down to me, and the lessons I learned through my experiences of yearning to be financially and spiritually free.

How to Use This Book

This book holds various methods and insight that I've used personally to help me along my journey to opulence. Some methods have been around for decades, while others I have personally created to help me break down various invisible walls. My aim is for you to constantly use this book to inventory and check specific areas in your financial and spiritual journey daily, monthly, and yearly.

You must not only read the book. You must live out the book. Test the methods daily. Apply each insight as soon as you read/understand it thoroughly. Document your progress. And then repeat it again and again until you know it by memory. Consistency is the key to success. You do not have to be considered brilliant nor a genius to see incredible results from this book. You just have to lean on your faith, apply the knowledge found within, and be patient. Preparation and timing are everything.

Another way to use this book is to have accountability partners during the process (if you are able to find a solid person or two). Some of us call these partners a mastermind group. At the start of my journey, I didn't have anyone to hold me accountable, because it was a personal decision to attain wealth in both my financial and spiritual lives. Because of this, I was aware that I would have to spend a lot of time by myself until I got to a level where I would attract people who would be thinking on my level, and they would introduce me to others with the same mindset.

So, if you aren't able to attract/find anyone at the moment, do not get discouraged. Just begin the process, and push yourself to be a better version of your current you. Trust me, you will change, and this book will help you in various ways to get acquainted and comfortable with that new you. Remember, this book is a guide to opulence. A guide is a person or thing that advises or shows the way to others, that directs the motion or positioning of something.

The Power in
Finding Purpose

2

The first thing one must understand is the power contained in having a vision for yourself. Often, people will take extraordinary leaps in their lives to achieve goals that they believe are aligned with a blurry vision. A person with no clarity of vision will perish in ways they wouldn't even imagine. Clarity is key. And with clarity comes effectiveness in decision-making, execution, and meaningful sacrifice. Clarity is power, and with power, you can clear your path of all the falsity to fulfill a purpose and mission that will make your life utterly worthwhile.

Vision Over Your Life

Here is something to think about: How you treat and see yourself is how you treat and see God. Before you can do anything of opulence, you must have a clear vision on where you want to go. You have to take an honest look at where you are currently and where you actually want to go. It is detrimental to state that you are expanding your land but currently have no clear picture of where you stand. A clear vision helps you to articulate what freedom means to you, what joy means to you, and what it is you are moving forward towards. Above all, it helps you know who it is you will be transforming into.

What is the real truth about yourself? Establishing a clear vision makes you take a deeper look into who you currently are. It helps you to recognize your truths and the lies you might be telling yourself (and others). What are the facts? You have to know the data on yourself. What we believe and what actually happens (or happened) can be totally different from one another. This is why having a clear and definite vision about your life will make things so much more productive and effective for you in the coming future.

You Control the Narrative of Your Life

A narrative is a spoken or written account of connected events—a story. You should be the only person giving that account as to where you are planning to go and what your overall vision looks like. Being alive lets us know that many chapters of our life story haven't been written yet and we have the power to create the outline of what we like to be told in the coming chapters of our life. We shouldn't be allowing others to dictate what our life's wealth should be because their vision wasn't the vision bestowed upon us. We control ourselves and we must control the things we project out into the physical world, because we will be the ones who have to live with consequences of our actions.

Hold Not to the Past, for Future's Sake

I won't assume that everyone currently reading this book has poor habits when it comes to their finances. However, if you don't have a healthy financial relationship and you constantly blame yourself for past mistakes, I encourage you to stop right now. You are going to have to purge yourself from the past so that you can focus on something much better. Where we live internally will manifest always in the external. What good is it to constantly dwell on what was, in the now? All it will do is keep you stuck in the present with the same results that you experienced in the past. You must let go of how you feel about what happened to you or what you have done. You can't change any of it. You are living the results of all the past actions right now. Acknowledge that. Give thanks for all those experiences. Then leave them right there, in the past. Whatever you have now financially, those are the cards you have to work with, however good or bad that hand is. Start where you are.

The goal is freedom, so that I can enjoy all the days and years of the life given to me.

The Life of
Order Chart

3

O n April 21, 2015, I was casted to be a background actor for the show *Law & Order,* in New York City. During the time waiting to go on set to be filmed, I envisioned how many years I would have if I were granted the blessing to live to be a hundred years old. Being that I was thirty-two at that time, I had sixty-eight years left.

But I went a bit deeper into the vision to get more clarity. I asked myself questions like, *How many summers will I have? How many years would I actually have to fly to other foreign countries? How many birthdays will I be able to celebrate in an actual nightclub? And how many years would I have to sacrifice to reach a status of financial wealth with what I'm doing now?"*

So, I wrote my age down, then created a two-column chart with years to reach an age on the left side and the age on the right side:

Age: 32

Years to Reach	Age
3	35
8	40
18	50
28	60
38	70
48	80
58	90
68	100

At that moment, it became clear that all those current decisions that seemed impossibly hard were actually easy to make. I saw the next ten years of my life become so clear that I started sharing with some of the fellow actors what I'd just created. Many of them thought that what I'd created was quite profound, while others asked me questions about what exactly the chart made me realize.

Over the years since I created the chart, I've referred back to it periodically to remind me that my time on this beautiful planet is very limited and fickle. Even though the chart shows that I had sixty-eight years to reach age one hundred, it doesn't guarantee that I will see that age. So it allowed me to see that I need to make decisions swiftly and effectively so that I can experience life at the highest capacity I possibly can. The goal is freedom, so that I can enjoy all the days and years of the life given to me. Even if I reach the age of one hundred, what I did in my twenties and thirties won't be what I can experience in my nineties.

So it is my hope that the chart I created for myself will also be a chart that helps you see your life a bit more clearly and moves you to make any decision you were struggling with, and makes that decision easier.

What do you want to accomplish, and where do you want to be in these highlighted years? If today was the last day of your life, would you want to do what you are about to do today? Before you move on in this book, let's get some real clarity on the time you have to experience life in certain ways. Just remember that nothing is guaranteed, not even the life we yearn to have. But we do have the opportunity to envision and pursue it in the best way we know how.

Age _____

Years	Age

Notes: After you have filled out the chart, just sit for a moment and reflect on how many seasons, holidays, birthdays, and big goals you can truly experience in the time frames you focus on. Think about the experiences that you could have.

Facts, Opinion, and Speculation

4

"*Those who do not remember the past*
are condemned to repeat it."
—GEORGE SANTAYANA

W hen it comes to building wealth, you must understand the difference between fact and opinion. During my years of studying wealth, I have received and heard some of the most outlandish and intriguing information in regards to attaining wealth. In this section, I wanted to make sure I am completely clear and direct with you about this.

Let's look at the terminology of the word "fact": a thing that is known or proven to be true. A fact is a piece of information used as evidence or as part of a report or news article. So remember that for it to be a fact, it must be *proven* to be true. All too often, people will make very important financial decisions based not upon facts, but opinions or speculations.

Let's take a look at both words, "opinion" and "speculation." The word "opinion" means a view or judgment formed about something, not necessarily based on fact or knowledge. So remember that this is just a *viewpoint* by one or more people. You get where I'm going with this yet?

Okay, so now, let's take a look at "speculation." This means the forming of a theory or conjecture without firm evidence. For example, providing reasoning to investment in certain stocks, property, or other ventures in the hope of gain but with no solid factual information or data is a form of speculation. This is nothing more than *theories* without evidence.

Having the facts is one of the most important things to remember when dealing with anything, especially your finances. You should not be making any financial decisions, large or small, without having all the facts. These facts come from doing the research, pulling data from valuable and credible sources (i.e. people, books, surveys, charts, historical references, etc.).

The late, great Nelson Mandela, former President of South Africa, once stated in his book, *Mandela: The Authorised Biography*, that when he was debating his highly intelligent friends, they could only debate using factual information and credible sources if they wanted to be strong contenders. What he stated is just as true when dealing with building wealth. You *must* make sure you know everything there is to know about the banks you will use, the businesses you are going to invest in, the advisors and mentors you will be getting insight from, and the sources that you will be pulling data from. If you want to build wealth, you have to do a thorough analysis of everyone and everything you will be attaching your money to so that it can work steadily for your benefit.

"Poor information is a liability
that creates poor people."
—UNKNOWN

You Must Rely on Your Own Research

You will meet many people who will try to give advice or a blueprint to achieving something they've never experienced themselves. However, you have to filter the advice that others give you or you can end up at a dead end. I will be the first to say that there were times where I would listen to people because they were my friends, family members, or even just a well-spoken, poor, righteous teacher. You have to stay away from opinions and speculations if you want to continuously climb your ladder. People will always try to tell you what the future will be like and why you should do this with your money or buy that property. If they are not a credible source and/or don't have solid data (facts) to back up their advice, just leave that opinion right next to them.

You do yourself a disservice when you make any financial decisions without doing thorough research, when you leverage your finances or decide to risk a lot based on a hunch. If you don't have the best information or someone advising you with the best knowledge, you'll make foolish decisions.

What Should You Do?

The credibility of your source of information is key for the enhancement and stability of your finances. You should always question everything thoroughly, and after you've collected all your facts, make a sound decision. I actually send up a prayer right before I make a financial decision, but that's me. Question the individuals who are talking to you about wealth and the moves you should be making. Don't feel ashamed, embarrassed, or uncomfortable. You have major goals to reach, and you're dealing with your livelihood. So you need to be asking the right questions, or you'll end up in the wrong spot. If someone told you that you need to invest your money in a community because the property value is going to soar in two or three years, you would be a fool to just buy the property without asking why they believe this. It doesn't matter if they have been in the business for twenty-plus years—you need to see what they're basing that statement on. What or who is their credible source? What are the plans that they've seen that you haven't? So again, do your own research, because it's one of the best action steps to making wealthy and healthy decisions for your overall achievement of goals.

It is unintelligent to take an opinion and make a decision as if it was a fact. If you continuously execute your plan using this method, you'll never become wealthy or see extraordinary growth in what you do. When someone tells you to buy something or invest in something because "they believe" it's the right call, that is a clear opinion. You must always verify your information—it's one of the smartest things you can do.

Leave Your Enthusiasm at the Door

It's understandable why a person would be enthusiastic and excited to be on the journey to building wealth for themselves or their family. But you have to remember that the road to wealth creation is a long journey for many. And when the road that you take actually gets you there, you'll have to deal with another road to keep what you've attained. That's why I advise you to curb your enthusiasm when you are doing the work. Sure, be enthusiastic when talking to someone about what to do with your finances. Just be thorough. One thing I learned from Wall Street veterans is that enthusiasm is a solid trait for many areas, but for them, it always, hands-downs leads to disaster when it takes precedence. Be excited about the fact that you made the personal decisions to achieve freedom. But be serious and thorough when doing the work. Jumping to conclusions and being enthusiastic about new information that causes you to take a leap (without thorough analysis) will create major setbacks.

Your Emotion
Dictate Your Finances

5

"Don't tell me where your priorities are. Show me where
you spend your money and I'll tell you what they are."

—JAMES W. FRICK

W hen I first embarked on my journey to
attain financial wealth (freedom), I always
had the idea it had a lot to do with money in general.
But I learned pretty quickly that I was barely scratch-
ing the surface with that theory. The building of wealth
has much to do with your emotions and physiological
makeup. Everything starts from within. Yes, all that
you will cultivate, attract, and attain financially will be
because of how well you manage *you*.

When you make a decision or commitment, it
is based upon what you have processed mentally and
emotionally. It is your psychology that creates the type
of lifestyle you had, have, and yearn to attain. The mastering of your mind and emotions determines the accuracy of your actions. World-renowned life coach Tony

Robbins has stated that your quality of life depends on the quality of your emotions you cultivate from within. You must have gratitude and appreciation. Not anger. Not resentment. Have excitement, passion, and grace. These are the qualities that move you with a deeper purpose as you take the journey to achieving financial wealth.

When you are dealing with your finances, what are the specific methods you are executing to leverage them for greater return? What are your rituals? It is what you do most often that brings you what you had, have, and will have. But this stems from your physiology and emotions. That's why it is vital that you do an inventory check of yourself and your finances every day—once when you start the day, and once at the end of that day. You need to actually see where your focus was for the day. Follow the paper trail and it will lead you to an honest conclusion about yourself for the day.

How your investments behave is not as important as how you behave. Your finances are allocated to where you are mentally and emotionally. If you are focused on gambling, then you will see your money be allocated toward the casino, lottery, or similar. If your focus is to get people to pay attention to you, then you will find yourself allocating your finances to shiny things just for a spotlight that will last for only a short period of time. Your best friend and your worst enemy, when it comes to your finances, will always be you.

Building wealth takes a special type of focus. When it comes to finances on any level, it's about 80 percent psychological, according to Dave Ramsey, the financial guru and founder of Total Money Makeover. It is also about forming new habits and thinking patterns. You can have all the financial knowledge in the world but it is your behavior that determines your financial stability. You're the driver. If you don't take responsibility for what you do with your knowledge, then just like a bank with no money, it is insufficient. You must know yourself fully to make sound decisions for effective financial management. You must recognize and be honest with what you do and do not know, where you are most strong and where you are most weak.

MIT Research and Your Financial Attitude

During my research, I was able to build some of my wealth strategies based upon the insights provided by MIT. Here is what I found:

- If you are impatient, you are more likely a spender rather than a saver or investor.

- People lacking considerable income or wealth are more likely to spend their refunds more quickly. *The data also suggested that low-income, lower-liquidity individuals tend to tie their consumer demands very much to their income.*

People who preferred to "spend now" rather than "save for the future" had three-fold greater spending.

Never forget that how you think or feel about finances has a direct effect on your behavior, which is your overall financial attitude. You can figure this out by honestly asking yourself the following questions:

- What do you think about investing?
- How do you feel about the stock market?
- What are your thoughts on creating additional income through rental property?
- Are you strong in balancing your personal and/or company's budget?

What's your retirement plan?

I can list fifty questions like this, but I'm sure you get the point I'm making about financial attitude. Those who are highly involved with their finances are the ones who are highly excited about going through the process. Their only core focus would be to constantly strengthen their financial literacy and make sure they are getting the most out of their money. This will come in the form of intentionally saving and investing intelligently. Take an authentic and passionate interest in your finances, and you'll know where every penny is going.

Manage Your Emotions or Else

Manage your emotions seriously when it comes to building your wealth. Be a critical thinker who invests and leverages their finances with profound confidence and patience. To do this, you can't take everything you see on television, read in the newspaper, and hear from "experts" as complete facts. Remember, you must question and research everything thoroughly. If you don't, your emotions may run wild and persuade you to make risky decisions. Being a critical thinker with the type of patience and confidence I'm referring to will help you find opportunities in challenging moments and navigate through seasons of financial drought.

Discipline is another key to managing your emotions and financial attitude. Having the courage to say "no" when other people are trying to persuade you to say "yes" to financial opportunities (that don't benefit you) goes a long way. Not allowing another person or group of people to govern your financial decisions and mindset is golden. Most people who tend to pursue financial wealth quickly realize that it's their vision, and most people around them aren't actively trying to reach that level of financial freedom. So, it is critical to watch how people and all things within your current environment try to play upon your emotions. Remember that your finances and how things around you behave are much less important than how you behave.

Ayn Rand once said that money is only a tool. It can take you wherever you wish, but will never replace the driver. This is true because a driver must know the car they're driving and where they want to go. It's a waste to have the opportunity to go somewhere but not have any directions. You end up wasting time and the benefit of enjoying the vehicle and seeing all the scenery along the route. Make an effort to know yourself, create a clear vision of where you want to go, and use every bit of your time to create a map to get there. You're the driver, and your finances are just the gas.

Mindfulness to Manage Your Emotions

Going through the processes, strategies, and personal transition to becoming wealthy has a dynamic impact on your physiological and emotional well-being. That's why it's important to learn how to quiet the mind so that you can hear your true inner voice. Just because you hear all these voices of suggestions in your brain after doing research, listening to all types of experts, or watching who knows what, doesn't mean you have to act upon them. You have to allow yourself time to sit and listen to them without becoming attached.

Personally, I tend to practice meditation and listen to soft classical music. I'll sit and let my mind bring forth all that is dancing in my head until it has all subsided. Another activity I do is jogging through nature. This gets me away from the common environments where

I do my wealth building. It allows me to detach and be one with myself. And this is what you must do. Create an environment or dwell in an environment where you can detach and listen intently to what is dancing in that brain of yours until it can't make another move. Add it to your daily routine just as you include breakfast, lunch and dinner in your schedule. The best ideas and decisions will come from your mindfulness sessions. Some have their sessions at four or five in the morning, before the world wakes up. Others have them before bed. Do whatever works for you. It has to be your sacred space and time, aligning yourself to be a better version of yourself, to manage your emotions and constantly remind you of the clarity of your vision and the effort you must put forth to make it a reality.

Where Are You Emotionally Right Now?

Periodically, you need to ask yourself, "Where am I emotionally right now?" Recognizing when your emotions shift and learning to pinpoint the source of those shifts is powerful in so many ways. Along with providing yourself the answers, you need to develop a set of rituals for your mentality, body language, and verbal language. Knowing where you are emotionally will help you understand your spending habits, the environments you are placing yourself in, and the messaging you are telling others directly (and indirectly). Where you dwell internally is more important than where you dwell externally. The external is a world that we cannot control or have certainty about. But we can control the internal and have certainty about what is going on within. We can control our emotional and mental state of being so that we can make the best out of what we experience externally.

Establishing daily rituals to develop your mind to move in a way that will attract financial wealth is important. When you are creating your rituals, ask yourself if whether or not the rituals you are creating or currently following are assisting you in managing, attracting, and creating more financial rewards to become financially wealthy. Ask the question: What will I have to be willing to do in order to create more income, build a stronger network, and speak the language of wealth?

Here is an example of a ritual I learned from Ramit Sethi, who wrote the book, *I Will Teach You to Be Rich*:

- Take fixed cuts off your paycheck and automatically spend them toward your goals.
- This is what he calls the "Conscious Spending Plan."
- Use 60% of your income to pay for fixed costs *(i.e. rent, utilities, food, and credit card bill)*.
- Then take 10% for investments (i.e. 401K, stocks, Roth IRA)

- Save another 10% for vacations, holidays, and unexpected costs.
- The final 20% of your money, you can spend however you want.

Now, what's awesome about this is that if my 60% can't cover all my fixed costs, it doesn't mean I need to cut back, but rather that I need to find or create another income stream so that I am able to cover everything. This helps you recognize what you need to do and what the issue(s) could be. For example, if you have debt, you know that your 10% for vacations will have to go straight to your debts, because you can't create wealth while still being in the hole—you are either looking to climb out of one and/or never have to go back into one for the rest of your life. This is why effective and intentional rituals are important for your mental and spiritual well-being.

Some other rituals can include:

- Spending thirty minutes a day reading a book on finances (i.e. investing, stocks, budgeting, accounting, etc.)
- Reviewing your spending activities before bed to see where you money was allocated to within the last twenty-four hours
- Speaking with a financial advisor once a month

- Reviewing your wealth-building notes in the morning for fifteen minutes
- Reciting affirmations
- Going through a checklist daily to make sure you are constantly taking the right steps toward your financial freedom
- Sitting with your family and teaching each other about money management

Suppress Ego and Greed

As you build upon the insights toward gaining wealth, be aware that you must keep your ego and that sin of greed on a short, tight leash. You have a financial goal to reach, and that's all good, but you don't want to fumble because you didn't know how to be humble. When your currency starts flowing in a big way, you don't want your emotions to get the best of you. You don't have to jump at every opportunity that comes your way, nor do you have to buy more than you need. If you're able to turn down attractive opportunities while keeping your ego and appetite in check, you'll save yourself many headaches in the near future.

You must always keep your financial future in mind so that you don't make present-day mistakes. Focus on what you have to put in during the years to come so that you don't make hasty decisions with your finances as soon as you have some room to spend. Greed is the silent and deadly killer of everyone's finances. You must keep a steady pace and keep your emotions in check. Always keep in mind what got you in the position to have a small piece of your big picture.

This is why focusing on enhancing your financial literacy as much as you can and mastering your emotions and behaviors is so important. The ability to postpone gratification for a bigger reward later is fundamental for those in positions of great wealth. Sacrifice what's good now so that you can reap the benefits of something much greater later. Like Warren Buffett says, "If you can't control your emotions, you can't control your finances.

. . . you can't be out here in the world dreaming of flying high while living in the hole.

Get Rid of
Debt with No Remorse

6

*"Never spend your money
before you have earned it."*

—THOMAS JEFFERSON

One of the major hang-ups in trying to build wealth is accumulating debt. No matter what an "expert" says, never believe that you can have financial wealth with debt hanging over your head. How can you have money when you owe someone money? You can't truly enjoy the fruits of any labor in its fullness when you know that you have to actually give it to someone else.

When I began to organize my debt list and compare it to my income stream, I knew I was in for a ride. That ride would tamper with my emotional and physiological well-being from time to time. Getting rid of debt is a great decision to make (if you have debt), but it will also be a day-by-day process. You will have to manage what you do and how you react to things so that you don't make unwise decisions that will take you deeper into bed.

The Book of Proverbs states, "My son, don't make yourself responsible for the debts of others. Don't make such deals with friends or strangers. If you do, your words will trap you. You will be under the power of other people, so you must go and free yourself. Beg them to free you from that debt. Don't wait to rest or sleep. Escape from that trap like a deer running from a hunter. Free yourself like a bird flying from a trap." Wealth isn't formed through debt-minded and poverty-stricken behaviors. If you believe that owing people, banks, educational institutions, and anything of the like is fine while trying to accomplish this wealth goal, you have another thing coming.

Relentless Action and Mindset

You have to have a relentless state of mind and behavior to get rid of debt. Each day comes with its own surprises, so you have to have a sense of urgency for clearing the amount you owe to other people and business institutions. Every single day, ask yourself, "How can I lower my debt today?" You have an amazing, dynamic, illustrious, and inspiring dream goal to achieve. And you can't be out here in the world dreaming of flying high while living in the hole. You're not that type of person. You are strong minded, focused, and relentless in your pursuit of something more than what you are currently experiencing.

The term relentless means oppressively constant; incessant. It can mean harsh or inflexible. All of these descriptions are exactly what you have to be to be when you decide to get debt out of your life. You have no room or time to dance with it anymore—it has to go as soon as possible. The longer it takes for you to get out of debt, the longer it will take you to truly experience financial freedom and wealth.

Stick to a Debt-Clearing Formula

Having a strict formula allows you to make the proper decisions without being so emotionally involved with the process. Having a strict formula could mean taking 10 percent of any income you receive and allocate it directly to your debt. You can line up your debt amounts from least to greatest, and begin to eat away at each one bit by bit. Remember that emotions play a huge role in your motions. You must think things through so that you can remind yourself why you are on this path, why you have to be relentless, why you are making all these major sacrifices.

You are responsible for your financial decisions, problems, and solutions. You have to know where all your finances are going, every day. Not once a week or at the end of the month—*every single day*. Dave Ramsey stated, tautologically, that if you want to live like no one else, you have to live like no one else.

It is your responsibility what you do with your finances. It doesn't matter how old you are, because no person reading this book has someone telling them how they should make their own money and how to spend it. Please don't blame your personal decisions towards groups of people and/or historical situations that you were never a part of as reasons why you can't take full responsibility for your personal finances. This is all on *you*.

Having a solid formula gets rid of all that talk and debunks any weak belief systems you may try to develop. You're thinking about, learning, cultivating, attracting, creating, and embodying wealth. You know where you are financially, and you know what you can contribute to lowering your debt amount. Start there and move your way up by bringing your debt down. Financial intelligence solves money problems, and creating or adopting a debt-clearing formula is using your financial intelligence. Problems only persist when you are not taking the time to develop and use your financial intelligence in its highest capacity.

Take an Oath to Commit

The explorer W.H. Murray stated, "Until one is committed, there is hesitancy, the chance to draw back, always ineffectiveness. Concerning all acts of initiative

(and creation), there is one elementary truth, the ignorance of which kills countless ideas and splendid plans:
that the moment one definitely commits oneself, then
providence moves too. A whole stream of events issues
from the decision, raising in one's favor all manner of
unforeseen incidents, meetings, and material assis-
tance, which no man could have dreamt would come
his way." It is important to know that becoming wealthy
means you have to take an oath to be committed and
let it be known that you will do whatever it takes to
achieve what most think is unachievable.

Along the journey of commitment to building
wealth, you will be tested constantly in ways you have
never been tested before. Your family, friends, business
partners, associates, strangers, mentors, mentees, and
even your inner voice will test the hell out of you. You
have to be willing to be comfortable saying no more
than often. You are going to have to explain to your
loved ones why you won't be able to attend certain
functions or pay for various things like you used to.
Commitment is a real action. Sacrifice is tangible. Your
lifestyle will have to change for a while. You can't be
out here partying like you used to. You have to study
the market instead. You can't be on social media for
multiple hours a day—you have phone calls to make.

Debt comes and sticks around when you lack commitment to managing your finances, create an unreal-
istic plan, or haven't made a true personal decision to
not live in poverty anymore. A leader with no vision

shall perish. You are the person leading your finances. It is you who is leading the conversation about what you would like to see your finances do for you. It is you who gives the yes and no to the person who is itching to take your money. Get rid of debt starting today.

Debts Will Destroy Relationships

"It's good to have money and the things that money can buy, but it's good, too, to check up once in a while and make sure that you haven't lost the things that money can't buy."

—GEORGE LORIMER

"The rich rules over the poor, and the borrower is the slave of the lender."

When we go into debt with someone, we create a master-slave dynamic that can become toxic. You should be very hesitant to ask someone for a loan, or to give one if it is going to put you in a hole. I learned that the best thing to do is give money away as a gift rather than a loan. We all can agree that there will be hard times and surprises all throughout life, so paying back money you owe to someone may not be as easy as how it was given to you. You should take the relationship and the discussion about lending very seriously. The Book of Proverbs states, "The rich rules over the poor, and the borrower is the slave of the lender." You don't want to be a borrower. Wealth means affluence. You have more than enough. You have to move past the behavior of borrowing, because when you do this to a friend or they do this to you, it will put the relationship in jeopardy.

One Debt at a Time

The key to knocking out debt continuously is *focus*. You should not be thinking about how to knock out all the debt at one time if your revenue stream or personal income doesn't allow you to. Be real with where you are and what you can actually do. Take baby steps, but take relentless baby steps! Knock out the smallest debt first if you must, and then proceed to the next one after it's been cleared. You will do this continuously until your debt amount is zero. Might it take a long time? Yes. Will you need patience? For sure. Will there be moments when you want to do something other than pay off these debts? Absolutely. But you must remind yourself of why you're doing this. You have to take responsibility for the fact that you put yourself in this hole and it will be you who will have to pull you out of it. But remember, you've got this, because financial freedom is so much more enjoyable than a life with debt.

Expand Your Means to Clear Debts

Often, we hear people tell us that we need to live below our means because that's what it will take to become wealthy. But that isn't a hard-core fact. We must expand our means to become wealthy. It is not financially intelligent to just live below your means and assume this is a big part of the puzzle. The reality is you must expand so that you have more than enough to allocate in a major way. This definitely goes for your debt as well. It is best to aim to bring in more income/revenue (means) so that you can deplete as much of your debt as possible. The more you can make, the more you do with your finances.

Budgeting helps you plan for a positive return or surplus. Creating a budget while searching for ways to expand your means is financially intelligent. This provides you with financial integrity and an understanding of another route to building wealth. When you do the opposite of budgeting for a surplus or positive return, you end up with a budget deficit. This means that you spend more than you currently make. Most people who end up in a budget deficit are those who don't budget well and pay no attention to their debt amounts. People who spend much more than they currently make will attract greater debt, which will make it much more difficult to get out of.

You must pay attention to all aspects when dealing with your finances, which include the money you currently owe to others. Choose to find ways to make more income and revenue. Be relentless in this pursuit, because it all helps the bottom line of getting out of debt. Once you free yourself from debt, all the money you were allocating to debt can now go into investments that you've been yearning to jump into with no dead weight (debt) over your shoulder.

Most of the time,
those who don't take
the time to self-evaluate
their behavior will
always make the wrong
assumptions about why
they are where they are.

Behavioral
Finance and You

7

I n this chapter, I really would like for you to understand how things shift when it comes to your finances. Most of the time, those who don't take the time to self-evaluate their behavior will always make the wrong assumptions about why they are where they are.

Much of my insight on behavioral finance comes from solid research, but also from taking time to sit and learn from Daniel Kahneman, one of the most influential economists in the world. A little background on him, if you're unfamiliar, is that he is an Israeli-American psychologist and economist notable for his work on the psychology of judgment and decision-making, as well as behavioral economics, for which he was awarded the 2002 Nobel Memorial Prize in Economic Sciences (shared with Vernon L. Smith). His research and findings challenge the assumption of human rationality prevailing in modern economic theory.

Now that you have been acquainted with someone with a brilliant mind, let me begin to share my insights and notes, and effective ways to navigate the road of behavioral finance. You see, because we have investors, professionals, and computers in the market, it is extremely difficult to make money using psychological assumptions when it comes to investing. What most people need to understand is that those whom we consider "financial professionals" don't know significantly more than individuals who invest by themselves. It's just that these professionals know how to interact with people within their industry and have a very small amount of info that individual investors do not have. This is why we tend to see professionals take advantage of others, because they have just a small piece of relevant information.

One of the most important aspects of the psychology of investing and decision makers combined is confidence and expertise. Confidence is the feeling or belief that one can rely on someone or something; firm trust. It's also a feeling of self-assurance arising from one's appreciation of one's own abilities or qualities. Expertise, on the other hand, means top-level skill or knowledge in a particular field, or providing expert opinion or commentary. When we talk about finances and investing, it is recognized that we tend to have too much confidence in both our opinions and our beliefs. The result of this is an excessive amount of spending and trading.

Here is something vital to understand—confidence is *not* a good indicator of accuracy when it comes to your finances and investing. Confidence is nothing more than the stories we tell ourselves and the imaginary dreams we tell others about ourselves. These stories and visions that we create have nothing to do with the quality of information we receive or know to be true. When it comes to our finances, it is best to know that we can only be as accurate in decision-making as the information and data we attain.

Expertise is something we know and the actual condition in which it's developed. The only way that expertise can be developed is if the environment is regulated. By regulated, I mean brought toward order, method, or uniformity. Expertise can be developed, for example, when you are playing basketball, soccer, chess, or spades (my favorite card game). These particular examples may have an extensive margin of chance, but they are still regularities.

The Two Conditions

Daniel Kahneman spoke of two conditions that drive expertise and confidence. The first condition is regularity, and the second condition is a great amount of practice. Regularity, as we know, is the quality of being stable and predictable. We know that certain actions would be considered usual, normal, and customary. But the second condition, a great amount of practice, is also highly important. Once you are engaged in extensive practice, you will need fast and immediate feedback. This will allow you to make whatever necessary changes needed to be a high-achieving expert. It is important to know the consequences of actions—the feedback has to be clear, rapid, and eloquent.

When these two conditions are not involved in the actions or decision-making, you do not have expertise or much of any valid confidence. That's why it is very important to do hard-core research on the individuals who claim to be experts in finance or any field that you meet them in. When you are looking for expertise, treat the search like you're investigating an artistic masterpiece—give it a deep-dive evaluation. Look at the provenance of their suggestions, ideas, and proposals (side note—provenance means the place of origin or earliest known history of something). Thoroughly question everything and every person claiming they have the best expertise. Where does their advice actually come from? Does it come from a credible source, or is it just an idea they formulated in their heads en route to seeing you?

The Essence of Rationality

When we deal with our finances or when we allow others to step in to advise us on them, there must be a fully comprehensive view of everything. There are so many people who deviate from doing this, which oftentimes results in financial hardships. Whether you are a rational investor or financial adviser, you should always compare the best and worst scenarios of every financial investment outcome to make the most

intellectual decision. This in itself is the general difference between standard economics and behavioral
economics.

Standard Economics

Standard economics forces us to think of economics
solely in terms of seeking profit, which refers to maxi-
mizing an individual advantage. This type of economics
is claimed to be driven by the utility of future wealth
(or discounted future wealth or present wealth).

Behavior Economics

Behavioral economics studies the effects of psychological, cognitive, emotional, cultural, and social factors
on the economic decisions of individuals and institutions, and how those decisions vary from those implied
by classical theory.

Here is something that I found quite interesting:

Behavioral economics is primarily concerned with
the bounds of rationality of economic agents. An economic agent is an actor (and more specifically, a decision maker) in a model of some aspect of the economy.
Typically, every agent makes decisions by solving a
well- or ill-defined optimization or choice problem.
Behavioral models typically integrate insights from

psychology, neuroscience and microeconomic theory. The study of behavioral economics includes how market decisions are made and the mechanisms that drive public choice. The three prevalent themes in behavioral economics are:

- **Heuristics:** Humans make 95 percent of their decisions using mental shortcuts or rules of thumb.

- **Framing:** The collection of anecdotes and stereotypes that make up the mental filters individuals rely on to understand and respond to events.

- **Market inefficiencies:** These include mis-pricing and non-rational decision-making.

When we discuss behavioral economics, agents are to be motivated by something other than gains and losses. Gains and losses are all temporary. And this is one of the main reasons why you must be motivated by something other than this.

Gains and losses occur daily, and they affect our behavior. Wealth, on the other hand, is a state of mind. If we only focus on the experiences and allow them to dictate our behavioral pattern in finance, we may end up broke and a living example of what a person becomes when they make important decisions based upon the current experience they are having.

It is best for us to be more rational in our thinking toward a delayed consequence. A person who makes financial decisions with a complete rational mindset has a very healthy comprehensive view over the entire situation. Most people would look at the financial activities separately, when they should be looking at the collective whole. Research shows that a rational person would sell very little compared to those who are not rational in thought.

A Rational Pill to Swallow

If you are the type of person who shoots from the gut in your decision-making, it would be hard for you to understand that we all are going to have a great amount of opportunities and gambles within our lifetime. They are not always going to be exactly the same, nor will they manifest the exact way you envision them to reveal themselves to you, but they will be able to give you the result you are looking for. This is why you should not have a preference for how you will receive opportunities or individual gambles. This is a limited way of looking at things, which is called "narrow framing"—a tendency to see investments without considering the context of the overall portfolio (or situation). People who narrowly frame tend to not see the big picture. They look at activities and problems in isolation, which is a very bad thing to do when it comes to your finances.

It is best to have a policy or guideline in place for how you would decide on which opportunity you would take as well as gamble. Any person who is rational with their finances would be close to risk neutral when you evaluate their guideline or policy for themselves or the person they are advising. In addition, the individuals who are steady in their emotional behavior (not wavering in decisions due to a temporary bad or good situation), become much more wealthy and are much calmer, in graceful balance with their emotions. This is because they aren't reacting to losses constantly as they occur—they have the long view in mind for attaining wealth.

Financial Hindsight

Hindsight means understanding of a situation or event only after it has happened or developed. It is hindsight that makes a huge impact on investment behavior (financial behavior). Only right after a realization of what has happened can a person make sense of it. Once a person makes sense of a situation, their financial IQ grows, they become wiser, and they can articulate the lesson that was learned from the experience.

Hindsight reveals and teaches us that there is something wrong with our current reality. There are many people who are highly intelligent and well informed, and yet they make the worst decisions or can't predict what actually will be happening, even in the near future. A great example of this is the recession and market crash that occurred in 2008. It wasn't predictable to the majority; we only learned in hindsight.

To illustrate this further, we can use the example of two individuals competing for an award. Imagine that at the beginning, they are generally seen as equal in knowledge, skill, and ability. But once one of them loses and the other wins, we make an immediate conclusion that the winner is much smarter and/or stronger than the other. Nothing can change our view, because we can analyze, look back, and connect the pieces as to why one was better than the other.

When you want to make a solid and positive impact on your finances, be sure you have a complete understanding of your financial situation. Make sure all data, insights, sources, etc. are absolutely factual. Even if results and outcomes don't reflect what you planned for, be swift in connecting the dots, analyzing what happened, and embracing the lesson from it. Be like currency—keep it moving forward, because time is one of the most valuable commodities. Don't waste a second of it.

. . . if you want to be
successful over a long period
of time, you must first focus on
creating value for others.

An Interview with Charles

8

I came across an interview with Charles Koch, an American businessman and philanthropist which was quite interesting. It was the first time I ever heard him speak because he rarely gives interviews. But something told me to sit and watch the interview with the lens of a young student trying to learn any and everything on the subject I have grown deeply passionate about. So below are my notes and my extended thoughts on various points he made in the interview.

Integrity

Integrity is something we must have, no matter what field we are in while trying to establish wealth. Mr. Koch states that if you want to make a quick buck, there are many ways to do it. You can cheat somebody, or misrepresent something; you can go and manipulate the political system to get an advantage, But if you want to be successful over a long period of time, you must first focus on creating value for others.

This is important to remember because over time, people will not bother to invest, create continuous opportunities, or assist in your longevity if you are not serving them in a way that brings them value. This is part of wealth building. Having integrity allows you to constantly invest in your future daily. It increases your value of character and shows that you are a person of growing stature. We will always seek out help for the overall vision we set before ourselves. If you move with integrity, there can be no doubt that over time, you will attract the necessary people and tools to build the wealth you want to have, both internally and externally.

> *"Long-term success starts with*
> *creating long term value for others."*

Just as much as Mr. Koch is making a statement about integrity, it goes beyond the exterior. You must have integrity for yourself. You must add value to yourself so that you can have long-term appreciation of yourself. What good is it to value others and leave yourself out of the equation? Don't you know that if you don't love yourself, there is truly no way you can express love to others? We receive and/or attract who we are. When we value ourselves, we are careful of whom we allow into our circle. Everyone may knock, but you should know that not everyone is welcome. We create long-lasting well-being when we hold ourselves accountable for serving ourselves in the highest form. Because of this, we need not seek on the outside what we know is already within us. Integrity equals value, and value equals long-term success and well-being.

Appreciate the Unpleasant Work

Mr. Koch talks very transparently about unpleasant work. He states that if you don't learn to do dirty work, if you don't learn unpleasant work by the time you are in your thirties, you won't know how to do productive work. Many of you who are reading this can agree based upon your own life and/or the lives of others you know. Many people don't appreciate the lessons in doing unpleasant work, but that is where you create your wealth in various ways. I've met many people along the way who believe that they can avoid or don't have to partake in unpleasant work. And if they do partake in it, they don't complete it with integrity and pride. Writing this book was sometimes unpleasant because of the amount of reading, research, writing, and typing I had to do. But still, I took pride in it. This book, like many of my past books, taught me patience, the art of staying focused, and the effectiveness one must have when dealing with people who were needed to make this book a reality.

Unpleasant work is what all those who accumulate wealth had the reasonableness to complete. Whether at a young age or currently, it will come to you in various forms. Wealth is not something that everyone attains, even though it is in everyone's grasp in some form. If someone defines their family to be their wealth, you'd best believe there will be a lot of unpleasant work that they will have to deal with to keep the family together. It's no different with trying to attain financial wealth. You will have to do some unpleasant work to make sure every penny, euro, pound, or peso is invested properly.

Creating wealth at every level will have some type of unpleasant work attached to it, however, the goal isn't to do unpleasant work for the rest of your life. Unpleasant work doesn't necessarily teach you work ethic. It teaches you how to work productively and how to work with others in mutual benefit. Attaining wealth on a financial or spiritual spectrum requires consistent, effective actions, and calling upon others when needed with the intent of also accepting that your progress is the teacher to those who are part of the movement.

One great tactic is to find someone that enjoys the work you find unpleasant. It is best to find what you're good at, do it well, and then minimize your personal time spent on what you're not good at. As I like to put it, outsource that sucker! If you don't like account-ing, then hire an accountant. Don't like working in the dirt? Then carve out a few hours each day to build that firm you always envisioned yourself being in. Graduate from the unpleasant work to the work that you would do every day until your heart stops.

Grateful for Everything, Entitled to Nothing

During the process of creating wealth in your life, you must be thankful and grateful for everything that you accumulated along the way. You must appreciate all your good and bad experiences, all the relationships you've had and the ones you currently have. The easy and hard lessons you learned along the way must also be appreciated. These things have shaped and molded you to be who you are today. Be thankful for everything, because at any moment you could lose it all. And that in itself is a hard pill to swallow.

Many people believe that they inherently deserve privileges or special treatment they didn't work for at all. I emphasize the word "believe" because many people you will meet will think that they are entitled to something. We can watch young adults (even adults) cause temper tantrums because they feel that they are deserving of something they never worked for. But we know that those who don't work for what they receive can have a lack of appreciation. But the fact is, we should just be grateful for all and keep in mind that we aren't really entitled to the things we yearn for, especially if we didn't put the time and efforts into achieving them. Living with gratitude rather than entitlement leads to wealth in our lives. Not because we feel we deserve to be wealthy, but because we move with a sense of thanksgiving and appreciation of all that has been. The process of getting to any level will take hard work, and no one deserves or should feel entitled to something they really haven't worked their butt off for.

The Universe Is Ordered

The physical world is ordered and governed by certain principles. No matter who you are, where you are from, how much money you have (even none), the color of your skin, or your age, you will never be able to change the laws that govern our universe. If you are going to be successful in the physical world, you have to understand the philosophy of science and the scientific method.

Mr. Koch, for example, studied all the great thinkers such as Einstein, Aristotle, Plato, Socrates, Descartes, and so many of their like. These individuals spent their lives searching for ways of life, recognizing the laws, finding methods for understanding, and allowing others to learn and achieve the unimaginable due to their findings and writings.

Attaining wealth in your lifetime will take some time and patience. But you must also be aware that there are rules, methods, laws, and principles that we all must abide by as well. For every action, there is a reaction. Whatever title we give ourselves comes with history and a responsibility. It's like an invisible crown that we must be able to have strength to pick up and wear in total devotion to the overall ruling of our land, which is governed by something much greater than you and me.

The Collective of Knowledge

During my studies of wealth building on a financial and spiritual level, I noticed that truth and effective tools are spread all over the place. They are spread out all over the world in the form of people, books, videos, and pictures. I was listening to Mr. Koch talk about innovation being a highly valuable key to success, and he stated that you have to get all the displaced knowledge together to cultivate innovation. Think about this for a second. When we bring a group of individuals together in one room to discuss what they are all knowledgeable in, the ideas, methods, and energy skyrocket. When you collect a vast amount of books to do research, you will gain some intriguing insight and data to cultivate ways of connecting dots and seeing what were once invisible strings.

Wealth may take patience, discipline, and radical focus, but it also takes a collective of knowing. Over time, you will become very innovative in your saving and spending. You will become innovative in your expression of a higher self. You will be innovative in how you live a lifestyle to sustain and constantly elevate in your status and mind a state of abundance and wealth.

Build a Culture of Challenge

Your lifestyle is your personal culture. It's the music you listen to and enjoy in private and public. The events you attend. The food you enjoy making and eating. The amount of times you exercise a week, as well as the types of exercises you enjoy doing the most. These may be general examples of the details of your life, but they collectively create and nurture your personal culture (lifestyle).

With all the things that we do, we can either be intentional in expanding or stagnating ourselves through certain details of our lifestyle. The circle we keep is a primary part in these moments of growth or stagnation. We *must* be challenged by our circle of friends and family members for healthy growth. If this is not so, if your people don't challenge you, then you will be stuck. And that sucks for you. When your advisors, mentors, circle of friends, and family members aren't challenging you, they aren't doing their job as true friends or relatives. You won't be doing your best work or job, because you allowed part of your lifestyle to be with those who lack the enthusiasm to push you to the next level.

You must be challenged continuously. It is a vital component in building your wealth so that you can experience various levels of freedom. You have to be skeptical, and you have to be committed to long-term results. Everything rides upon your strength to carry and release the things necessary to experience a level higher than where you are. You must always push past your normal and average way of achieving things. We are building wealth. You have to think higher, move differently, and constantly be challenged by those who are going to prepare you to attain and sustain on a new level.

The Focus of Safety

Safety is the key and the number-one focus. When it comes to financial risk, you must evaluate the probability of success. You must ask the following question: What is the downside, and how does it compare to the upside? The upside is not just about the return on investment, but it will also build you a new capability or platform for growth.

Questions to Ask Yourself Continuously

- What do I truly want?
- What are my capabilities to create superior value for others and myself?
- What are the best opportunities for me to create value?

Remember: You must be constantly innovating for expansion and growth.

Look within to find the answers. Look within to see the glory of your kingdom and how vast it is . . .

You Are
the Living Word

9

Your power has and will forever be within you. Your thoughts become words, and all that you project in this world is the living example of all you think and say. Look within to find the answers. Look within to see the glory of your kingdom and how vast it is and can become in the physical world. You are the truth, way, and light when you step into the position you were destined to fulfill. You become the truth because you will live out all that you thought and spoke. You become the way because those who are seeking to be free from their personal bondage can look at you as one of the living blueprints to follow. Your process and achievement will be the inspiration that liberates others, near and far. You become the light because you found the outlet that you needed to plug into so that you can receive energy from the higher source. You will also serve as the light for those who are lost in darkness.

Your words are powerful, and you must speak life over your own life. You must also remember that the tongue mirrors the heart, and out of the mouth the heart speaks. Like water, whatever your heart is attached to, it will flow out like the Nile River. So be mindful of the thoughts and words you create and release into the universe. The universe is always listening and adding what you say into the fabric of your life. This will be revealed in the pattern of your words through your actions and way of living.

Be intentional with your words and those you allow to speak over and about your life with their words. Your life is rare, and when you speak, you can create incredible wonders and monuments for those around you to admire. So don't take your life for granted. You are a living testament to the storms you calmed and the peace you created from within. You walk in grace, and all that you create from within can be spoken and birthed into this world.

The Radical Way
of Doing All Things

10

Radical Vision and Thinking

R adical is a word I fell in love with a few years ago. It was a moment in my life where I knew that I needed to make a change. I knew that a breakthrough had to happen, but the first step was to recognize what part of my life was in bondage. We all have been in some type of bondage, and when we get sick and tired of being sick and tired, we start to take the initial steps to getting better (having a major breakthrough).

Radical became my word of encouragement and motivation. It was the word that made me think of what could be if I dived straight into the ocean of change and shedding of old ways. I knew that for a breakthrough to happen, I had to make the first step in releasing old ways, habits, and stagnant relationships so that I could grab hold of healthier ones. I know that we cannot be 100-percent committed to the change we needed within and around ourselves if we keep tampering with unhealthy situations and our past. And we can sometime be layered with many things from our past

Radical means relating to or affecting the fundamental nature of something; far-reaching or thorough (especially of change or action). The fundamental nature of what I wanted to change was the thoughts and visions I had about my life. When we are fully grown, we honestly can't blame anyone for how we live on this planet. Yes, there could be factors that could help or hinder us at times, but when you look at it, we are beautiful and brilliant human beings who are capable of stepping away or stepping into the bullshit we experience.

We need radical vision and radical thoughts to push beyond what we see. Years of toxic and hindering belief systems need to be broken down with a radical mind. You can be thinking on the same level as some garbage you've been exposed to. You need to think higher, move faster, speak louder, see farther, and dream well beyond what others tell you is amazing. The one who is a radical visionary and thinker seeks to see what is outside of the box they have been placed in. They seek to shift it. They seek to look at it differently and expand it so they can add the most valuable things within it.

You must look beyond what you see in this current moment. There is nothing normal about where you are. There is nothing normal about knowing that your bondage is your safe haven. Get out of here with that mindset! Your normal is to live among or beyond the stars. Your dwelling place is well off in the lands that many can't even see within their minds. You see, you will meet more than enough people who will never be excited to think radically, create radical visions, or take actions in the most radical manner. These people may fit your preference, but they for sure don't fit into the promise or purpose that is set over your life. The radical-minded person will question all that is around them. They will ask if their relationships and activities are conducive to a radical vision. Ask yourself: Will they add or take away from the drive I have to accomplish the ever-so-radical promise and purpose over my life?

When we decide to live radically, it can be scary at first. We are excited, but we are also nervous wrecks. We don't really know what to expect, because it's all new to us. Many things begin to change around us. We are moving at a higher frequency. Our energy has to stay at an all-time high, constantly. There are shifts happening all around us and we, of course, can be a bit frightened by the unknown. But not to worry— this is all going to work out in your favor. The process of something this extreme and new in your life will have you feeling like you're on a daily roller coaster. Put them hands up, yell at the top of your lungs, and laugh hysterically.

Radical Actions

Nothing can change unless there is action. Knowledge is nothing if it's not applied. There is a bible verse from the book of Ecclesiastes 12:12 that says, *"But, my child, let me give you some further advice: Be careful, for writing books is endless, and much study wears you out."* We must be radical in our actions. We must be relentless, because breaking habits we formed decades ago is going to take some serious willpower. It's going to take a powerful mind, vision, and person of action to attain something special in their life.

Radical Action is doing something you probably do right every day and intensifying it. For example, I would do 200 push-ups four to five times a week. Then I pushed myself to do 300 push-ups. But when I decided to be radical in mind and action, I started to do 500 push-ups, still three to four times a week. I also went radical in my morning runs. Instead of doing three miles, two or three times a week, I decided to do five miles, four times a week. I wasn't and I'm still not playing games when I decide to live radically. Think about where you are in your life. Look at what is working and what isn't doing anything. Starve the weak things, intensify the good things, and watch how the results will astonish you.

When you make the decision to be radical in your actions, you are setting yourself up to receive some of the most unimaginable blessings, but you will be testing the core of all your belief systems. Your faith will be rocked and shaken like never before. People will think you are crazy and even laugh at you. You're probably laughing at what I'm saying right now, but watch what I say to you. People are going to say the most off-the-wall things about you, because your actions aren't "normal." They will be unconventional and unorthodox. But don't let that deter you. Extraordinary will be your ordinary. You will live in the land of the unfamiliar and be the familiar sun that shines in that unchartered landscape, all because you applied yourself. You pushed your human spirit to create your version of heaven on earth as the creator that you are.

I remember watching and listening to Tyler Perry, an American actor and producer, speak about individuals who have dreams and immaculate visions. He made the following statement, which I believe resonates with being radical. Now, I'm not trying to be all spiritual with you during this time, but just read and take in what he is saying about people like us who push the envelopes and boxes to see the unseen:

> *Sometimes when you follow God, things get tough and they get tight. But if you keep pushing, on the other side, something miraculous will happen and change your life. Something will open up and blow your mind.*

Doesn't matter how many people love you, care for you, hate you, or try to take you down. When God has a dream for you, it is your dream. Your dream.

And there are people who love you and think they are saying the right things for you to try to protect you, or there are people who have been in your lives and watch you grow up but don't know the dream that God has put down inside of you, because they think they are too familiar with you. But what you have to understand is that when God has something fully for you, you have to go at it fully.

We have to be unapologetic but intentional with our radical way of thinking and our actions. Play out the entire movements and conversations that you will be having in your head first. Before you make any major moves, see everything play out in your mind. See the facial expressions, the season, the outfit, the colors around you. Feel the emotions of what it will be like as you take those leaps, relying on your faith. Recognize who you want with you and what their statements will be. Confirm how you will respond and the mannerisms you will show. This is the power of radical thinking, radical actions, and accomplishing radical results.

Carnegie Hall | The Radical Move

On September 21, 2017, I achieved something that would have been beyond my normal, until I decided, two years prior to the event date, to live radically. That achievement was headlining a sold-out lecture at the world-renowned Carnegie Hall in New York City. It was transcendent on so many levels, and here are the reasons why. Exactly two years prior to that radical date, September 21, 2015, I was at Carnegie Hall attending an event to see a famous pianist. When I walked into the hall where the show would take place, I was blown away by the beautiful space. How could I not take a picture from the back of the room to have as a keepsake? My girlfriend at the time just smiled and knew I was in my happy place. I watched as everyone came in dressed and excited. There were so many whispers and such high energy just at being in the room. As we waited for the show, I showed her the picture and then it hit me. I immediately said to her, "What do you think of me having a lecture here? I don't think something like that has ever been done. What do you think?"

She said, "I think you should look into it. It would be awesome, Rah."

At that very moment, I knew that I could do it. I could see it happening. I was obsessed with the idea, the vision, and the emotions that were running through my entire body. When I got home, I spent some time going through the entire website, writing notes, and even sending out an email to the event coordinator before bed. The next day, I received the response with all the pricing and details that were needed to plan.

Notes:

- You *must* be obsessed with the vision to see it through.

- There will be many moving parts throughout the process of making it a reality, so being obsessed can help you to deal with whatever comes your way.

- See and get all the details together to master the process and make the moment one to remember.

Once I had all the details, I spent the next few days planning out the entire show. When all was completed from what I viewed on the paper, I reached out to the event coordinator to set the date. I was excited and thrilled, until she said I would have to wait until January to see if the date would work. But it was currently going into October, and I wanted to lock in a date right then. This is what happens when you are moving radically; things will be on a high until you hit a red light moment. It is only then that your focus, willpower, and faith will begin to be tested. She said she would write down the dates I wanted (the second or third Wednesday of February 2016) and get back to me at the beginning of the New Year.

Four months went by, and I had to continue to keep the vision alive and keep my enthusiasm up, because even though there are no guarantees in life, I know that we must always choose to have radical faith that what we envision will work out in our favor.

So, January comes along and nothing happens. No phone call or email. I got an email late in January, and I had to be aware that they didn't finish completing their season calendar so they couldn't let me know when I would be able to get the date. So we pushed the date back to late August/September. All I had to do was leave a deposit to secure the date, but that wasn't possible at the time because I was preparing for a tour and my funds were tied up in many things. So I ended up telling her that I wasn't ready and I would try again next season. A full year of practicing radical faith, radical thinking, radical action, and radical vision, all while doing other impactful things. It took a lot out of me when I came to realize that the timing was not aligned. When I spoke with the event coordinator, she was very understanding and stated to me that it would happen and she looked forward to keeping in touch for the following season.

It was a bit devastating, because with all the blessings that were happening around me, I knew that this vision was the radical test of my belief system and brilliance. How would I make this happen? This was the question every single day. Then I decided to speak life constantly into my vision. I surrendered and got rid of any doubt that might have danced in my head. I kept my faith strong and the vision as one of my top priorities to achieve. I knew that when the time was set, it would happen.

Fast forward another year later, and it did happen. And it happened exactly on the date that I took the picture back on September 21, 2015. I was able to receive a paid speaking contract to use part of the funding as a down payment on the venue, then spend almost seven months promoting the event as the final stop on my global tour entitled "Skyscraper." Everything was aligned—my old high school honored me during the same month, and then the School Board sponsored two charter buses of students to attend the event. Then the EOF program that assisted me in getting into college sponsored a group of students, and then various programs and people that supported me over the years purchased tickets.

Two weeks before the night, we announced that every seat in Carnegie Hall was completely sold out. Talk about radical. Friends and family flew into New York from different countries, states, and cities. All I could do was walk on the stage and cry with tears of joy. And then the unbelievable happened—when I said my last line, stating that "My location was not my destination," the crowd gave me a standing ovation.

There were so many elements that should be in this storyline, but I just wanted to share this story with you, because I am a living example of what radical living can bring you. It won't be an easy start, but the feeling will be extraordinary from the beginning. You will have to surrender to a higher power, one greater than you. You will have to acknowledge and understand universal laws. You will need to be aware that you will not fail, but you will fall. And as long as you are sure that you will always get up, you will succeed in the most incredible way.

Your standards will change, and so will your surroundings. Your conversations will change, and so will the people you are around. Your focus will change, and so will the views you see. Your money will change, and so will your habits. But believe me, opulence will be yours, as well the land it dwells in.

Photo Credit: Baa-ith Nurri-Deen

Be Your Radical Best

I had the opportunity to listen to Nastia Liukin, who is a Russian American former artistic gymnast. She is the 2008 Olympic all-around champion, a five-time Olympic medalist, the 2005 and 2007 world champion on the balance beam, and the 2005 world champion on the uneven bars. She is also a four-time all-around U.S. national champion, winning twice as a junior and twice as a senior. With nine World Championships medals, seven of them individual, Liukin is tied with Shannon Miller for the third-highest tally of World Championship medals (among U.S. gymnasts). Now that you have received a short introduction, I wanted to share some of the insight she provided about what we need in order to be the best at whatever it is we do. As I am discussing being and living radical, I figured my notes from listening to her would be most effective.

We must promise a pact to ourselves to do everything possible, absolutely everything, so that when we look back, we don't have a single regret.

We have to try our hardest to be our personal best. There are no excuses. We have to double up on things so that we can be the smartest, healthiest, most creative, and highest version of ourselves.

We must not compete with others, but rather be the best version of ourselves compared to who we were last year.

Do not hold back! Give it your all in every way possible!

Train every single day, and believe in yourself just like you believe in God.

Your awards don't mean anything! You are so much more than those awards. Do not let them define you, by any means. Don't display or flaunt them. Stay focused on the process.

Defer gratification (That's it . . . what more do you want me to say?) The focus is the work. The process. The impact.

Let's be clear, you will have days where you want to quit this radical journey ,but don't you do it! Stick with it no matter how hard it becomes. How you react is on you, because you can't control the situation, just how you react to it.

What do you think about yourself when you're by yourself? This is an important question to ask, because you are who you are when you are by yourself. Do you see yourself as a failure? A winner? A doubter? Peaceful? Brilliant?

Remember that what you want to do is in your control. Don't follow what society believes you should do. Do you! Know your end goal and plan it out. Set the date, and then work backward on your strategy. Create the path to get to the end goal by a specific month.

*The two
things that are important
when it comes to investing are
time and knowledge. But of the
two, knowledge is king.*

Value in Investing

L et's get straight to the meat of this section, because time is valuable and we don't have any to waste. Investing means expending money with the expectation of achieving a profit or material result, by putting it into financial schemes, shares, or property, or by using it to develop a commercial venture. It also means to provide or endow someone or something with a particular quality or attribute.

Please be aware that two things are very important, but one tops the other in a strong way. The two things that are important when it comes to investing are **time** and **knowledge**. But of the two, knowledge is king. Still, we need to appreciate both and recognize how both play a part in helping us become highly effective and impactful investors in our financial and personal lives.

Time Reveals All Things in Due Time

Information is powerful leverage when we are trying to build up ourselves, our finances, or other individuals. But information that is not used at the right time can be ineffective and obsolete tomorrow. Whether we're talking about the world of money or our personal world, it is all fluid, ever changing. Time will reveal if you had the right information for an early investment or if you missed the mark and made a late investment. We, as investors, must always stay in the flow of receiving new and relevant information so that we know when to make the right decisions and investments, at the right time.

You must constantly question yourself about where you are getting your information so you can stay on point with your research. You have to continue to do the necessary work and research so that you invest effectively and gain as much money as you possibly can. It may annoy or irritate people when you ask them what their source is. But your time and money can't be given away so easily. Know that everything about you—mind, time, and grind—is a rare jewel.

Valuable Questions to Ask Yourself

You might have read in my previous books that it's important to inventory check yourself. This is something that must be consistent and part of your daily routine. For example, I wake up every morning and check all my accounts (business/personal), debt amounts (if I have any), and current and potential revenue streams. I make note of the long-term, short-term, and current-day goal(s). I play no games with this habit. I don't care if others say it's not necessary. If this makes me highly effective with building my wealth, then the opinions of men can dive off the deep end with a boulder strapped to their feet. Drown the opinions of men with no remorse.

The questions you must ask yourself are:

- How near am I to the source of this information?
- How credible is this source for the information I received?
- How can I leverage this information for the biggest impact on my investments?

Remember: The more credible your source and the closer you are to the source, the more achievable your goal of becoming wealthy.

There is a famous line from my favorite television show, *House of Cards*, that plays well with what I say about being close to the source to make sure you have the most accurate information and knowledge. *"Power is a lot like real estate. It's all about location, location, location. The closer you are to the source, the higher your property value."*

Keep the Currency Flowing

The dollar died in 1971. Yeah, it died over forty-five years ago, and people are still acting like they still have it. Let me help you switch your dead mindset and how you are valuing something that's not here. We can sometimes forget that nouns change. Yes, nouns! People, places, and things! When the dollar was no longer relevant, it became all about currency. Currency means a system of money in general use in a particular country. It also means the fact or quality of being generally accepted or in use. I like to think of currency as its sibling, current, which means belonging to the present time; happening or being used or done now. Currency, your money, like the current of a river, must keep moving to keep its value. So wherever you move your currency to, it should be towards sound investments with the intention of receiving a positive return on your investment in the near future. But if the value of your currency becomes less due to poor or bad investment, your currency will not be appreciated or accepted by others.

Know the Rules

Investing should be made when you are fully knowledgeable of the rules, have a great circle of advisors, and have sound information on all things you want to invest in. So many people who consider themselves "investors" in some capacity tend to lose a lot and find themselves in burdensome situations because they didn't leverage the knowledge they received or the brilliant advisors they attracted, nor did they abide by the rules that were specified in the beginning of their investment journey. No matter if you are investing in your self-development, your financial growth, or the lives of others, you have to be highly resourceful and fully engaged in making the most effective decisions and moves in the least amount of time. This can only happen when you spend the time to understand and maximize all your tools/resources.

Know the Trends

The term "trend," as defined by the Collins Diction-ary of Business, means the direction of movement of a variable such as sales over time. The dictionary goes on to say that a trend is a broad change in attitude and behavior in society over time. These can serve to influence the acceptability of products by consumers with some products going out of fashion while others become more popular. When you take a collective of facts and make an opinion about a consistent behavior, this becomes a trend. It's dynamic if you have a solid source of information from various areas and can truly understand it. When you can apply the information and make a proper decision with an investment, your moves are highly intelligent.

A Little Can Do More Than Much

Don't believe the hype that you need to be making six figures to get started becoming a millionaire. Do you know that there are people who earn six figures but have never been (or will never be) financially wealthy? Do you know that there are people who made much less than six figures but became financially wealthy?

The difference between these two groups is their disciplines, belief systems, and how they leveraged the information they both received. It's not about the color of your skin, religious background, sexual orientation, or the community you grew up in. Cut that out of your thought process right now. You must be built for attaining wealth by investing in a healthy mindset and habit that has stood the test of time and made many people wealthy in their own right.

Information, Mindset, and Technology

Information is your golden egg. People tend to forget that information can be the lifeline or death sentence to a wealthy lifestyle. It is also the big difference in terms of who will be wealthy or poor. Just have the right information so that you can transition from being poor to wealthy or continue to maintain a wealthy life. Information, leverage it with technology, can aid in achieving great financial wealth over time.

Warren Buffett's Six Wise Rules to Investing

One of my favorite K-Studies during my wealth creation process has been with Warren Buffett. I have attended his Shareholders Meeting in Omaha, Nebraska to watch-some of the most valuable interviews he's ever given from back in the early 1980s. Warren is unarguably one of the most valuable teachers of wealth and life lessons in this lifetime. The first pair of rules I learned from Warren when it came to financials, specifically with investing was:

Rule #1: Never lose money

Rule #2: Never forget Rule #1

After years of studying and researching Warren, Here are six wise rules that I was able to pick up and leverage in multiple ways. He started talking about these rules in 1985, but trust me, they are still relevant today.

1. Buy Below Intrinsic Value
2. Managers Must Have a Fact-Driven Temperament
3. Study the Business; Not the Stock Price
4. Don't Give In to the Hype
5. Only Buy the Things You Understand
6. Don't Overcomplicate Investing

Buy Below Intrinsic Value

Warren stated that the first rule in investing is to not lose money and the second rule is to not forget the first rule. Those are the only "two" rules that need to be acknowledged and respected. If you buy things for far below what they are worth and you buy a group of them, you won't be losing money.

Money Managers Must Have a Fact-Driven Temperament

Warren stated that an investment manager's most important quality is their temperament. Investment is a temperamental quality, not an intellectual quality. You don't need a high IQ in the investing business. You just need a stable personality, a temperament that derives great pleasure neither from being with or against the crowd. This isn't a business that takes polls. It is a business where you just have to think. Warren went on and stated that Ben Graham, his long-time mentor and advisor, would say, "You're not right or wrong because thousands of people agree with you or disagree with you. You're right because your facts and reasoning are right."

Study the Business; Not the Stock Price

Warren was asked, "What do you do than 90 percent (or most) money managers in the market?" He
responded by saying, "Most professional money managers focus on what the stock market will most likely
do for the next year or two. They make up all types of
opinionated methods to approach that, but they don't
think of themselves as owning a piece of the business.
The real test of whether you are investing from a value
standpoint is whether or not you care if the stock
market is open or closed tomorrow. If you are making
a good investment in securities, it shouldn't matter if
they close the stock market for five years." He went
on to say, "The ticket only tells you the price, which
we can look at occasionally, but prices can't tell us
anything about a business. Business figures can tell us
something about a business, but not the stock price."

Warren would rather value a business (or stock)
first without knowing the price so that he isn't influ-
enced by the price when making his evaluation. And
only after all this will he then look at the stock price to
see if it's in alignment with what his evaluation is.

Don't Give In to the Hype

Warren likes a lack of stimulation (not with emotions)
when dealing with investing or finances as a whole.
He believes the focus should be to get facts and not

personal stimulation from outside sources trying to hype you up about where to invest your money. There is no need to have a bunch of people in your ear. Warren said that if he were on Wall Street, he would be a lot poorer, because someone can get overstimulated in that type of environment. You'll hear lots of things, and that can shorten your focus. And a short focus is not conducive to long profits. It's best to dwell where you can just focus on what businesses are actually worth. We have to remember that this is an intellectual process, and the less static there is within the process, the more effective and better off you are.

Only Buy the Things You Understand

Warren stated that intellectual process is defining your area of competence in evaluating business. And then, within that area of competence, find whatever sells at the cheapest price in relation to value. He made it clear that we do not have to make money at every game. "There are all types of things I know nothing about. That may be too bad, but why should I know all about them? I haven't worked hard on them," said Warren. "In the securities business, there are many companies willing to sell you a piece of their business, which changes daily. Nothing is forced upon you, and you don't have to invest in all of them."

"It's like a baseball pitch. They pitch to you every
day, and you sit there all day and hit not one, or hit
only the ones you know you can really hit."

——WARREN BUFFETT

Don't Overcomplicate Investing

The act of being patient in this process of investing can
be boring. Boredom is the problem with most money
managers and investors. The method of investing is so
simple, and the reason why everyone doesn't follow
it is because of their academic focus on everything.
People pay attention to all types of variables because
the "data" is there. But what they don't realize is that
"data" can be manipulated. If you are patient enough,
what true will become revealed to you. And then, you
invest in the most informative and effective way.

"To a man with a hammer,
everything looks like a nail."

——WARREN BUFFET

Once people have these "skills" or data, they are
antsy to use them whenever and however they can. But

they aren't important, Warren tells us. If Warren were asked to purchase a business, it wouldn't matter if he purchased it on Saturday or Tuesday. This isn't what a businessman thinks about when looking to buy a business, so why think about it when buying stocks? Cause stocks are just pieces of a business as well.

Everything Is Energy

12

W hen on the course of reaching a level higher than where you are, you must be aware that everything around you is energy. Your finances move toward where you focus your energy. If you like shoes, you will direct your energy in the form of currency toward buying shoes. If you are a foodie, you will definitely direct your energy toward trying new dishes, no matter the cost from time to time. People who are highly infatuated with someone may show this in the form of spending their currency toward what that person likes, even very expensive items. Just as we have been talking about the terminology of "currency," we must remember to treat it as another expression of energy that is always moving due to the behaviors of individuals like you and me.

Currency to me is like the term "*current*." Current is a flow of something in a particular direction to a specific place. When we direct our attention to something we like and it has a price tag on it, our actions and currency flow directly to that target, just like a natural current. When we don't allow our money to act as a current in our lives, it will be like a puddle of water on the hottest day of the summer season and dry up.

Diving Deep about Energy with Dandipani

Even though I touched upon the energy behind currency, it still is in direct connection to the energy that you and I cultivate and distribute out into the world. I want to share with you some of my insights and some of the most profound teachings and understanding of energy by Dandipani. If you don't know, Dandapani is a Hindu priest, entrepreneur and former monk of ten years. He has accumulated many prestigious awards from various high-profile companies and organizations from around the world. Listening to him speak about energy confirmed for me that what I was thinking, teaching, and observing was of divine alignment. Here are some of the notes that I hope you will be able to apply in your daily focus of wealth creation in various parts of your life.

Dandipani said that we must look at energy the same way we look at water. Water is sprinkled across land to help it grow flowers and weeds. The same goes for energy. Whatever we put our energy toward (positive/negative) it will all grow just the same. Like water, energy doesn't have the ability to discriminate. We, right now, are the sum total of where we invest our energy throughout our entire lives.

Dandipani goes on to say that as a monk, there are two important areas: the awareness and the mind. Our energy goes wherever our awareness goes. If we have a moment where our awareness is on anger, our energy will intensify in that direction. Every single day we allow people to dictate where our awareness goes, and as a result, we place our energy there too. The manifestation of all that we see in our lives comes from where we allow our energy to flow. One thing that Dandipani stressed was that the goal isn't to control your mind, but to control where your awareness goes *within* your mind throughout the day. To do this, you must learn and master the art of concentration, keeping your awareness on one thing for an extended period of time.

Concentration should be practiced by doing one thing at one time every day.

QUESTIONS TO ASK YOURSELF

What is an event/result that happens constantly in my life?

What is a recurring event?

There are tools that we can use to disrupt or change a recurring event in our life. We don't have to complicate things. All we have to do is insert a tool such as meditation, prayer, concentration practice, or something of the like.

Develop Your Willpower for Great Energy

1. Finish What You Begin
2. Finish It Well Beyond Your Expectations
3. Do a Little More Than You Think You're Able to Do

All three of these actions require effort, and that effort is willpower. Take these three things and apply them to recurring parts of your life.

Where Awareness Goes, Energy Flows.

Learn to Manage Energy in Your Life

Most people don't take the time to evaluate who and what they are investing their energy into. We have to treat energy the same way we treat money. It's a finite resource that needs to be managed, allocated, and invested wisely. Remember this: energy *cannot* be created or destroyed; it can only be transferred or transformed.

We all know that we have a finite number of years on this planet. Knowing this, we must be completely clear on where we want to focus our energy. We don't have the luxury of giving our energy to everyone.

Ask yourself what you want out of life. What are your passions? Make time to get to know yourself.

Energy Consumers

Dandipani states that there are three types of people:

1. Uplifting people
2. Neutral People
3. Not-Uplifting People

There are two ways to know if they are energy consumers:

1. Judge (based upon image, not interaction)
2. Evaluate (spend time with and come to a conclusion)

Other Types:

- Transenergy People – Those who give energy based upon conversation or the feeling they are having.

- Inherently Energy Consumers – Those who have always been this way, always taking energy since the beginning.

How to Deal with Energy Consumers

- Practice the art of being affectionately detached but always kind, gentle, sincere, and loving toward them. An example is when you meet someone, you say hello but don't ask "How are you doing?" because you are detached and it's not in your best interest to know. Keep it short and don't accept or give an invitation to meet again (especially over food).

Remember: People tend to say things they don't really mean and ask questions they really don't want the answers to. Stay aware of the energy being sent your way and the energy being asked for.

Place the burden of responsibility on the energy consumer. As an example, if someone asks for your time to pick your brain, give them your email address and tell them to send questions and you'll respond when you get it.

Every year, evaluate the people in your life and reallocate your energy between people who uplift you and those who don't. Your experiences have emotions attached to them; when you relive them or write them, they go from your subconscious to your conscious

mind. For example, energy (emotion) can be transferred to paper (i.e. a love letter or a birthday card).

NOTE TO YOURSELF:

To know yourself is the greatest gift to yourself.

Don't pursue the energy of happiness; pursue a
lifestyle that results in the energy of happiness.

You have to be building

for the long haul and not

simply the right now.

Play for the Long-Term Rewards

13

Mastering your finances, power, and mindset is not a process that should be looked upon as a game. This should be taken as seriously as if you heard about someone putting their life on the line for others. How you conduct yourself on this path to wealth is all up to you. The energy, focus, frequency, vibration, appreciation, and seriousness you give to this vision will show their faces throughout the journey. You have to be building for the long haul and not simply the right now. Those who plant seeds effectively and daily in the right now will have an abundant harvest in the future.

All those you have heard of or seen in real life who attained wealth did not focus on just the present moment. They looked at what they had as resources and asked themselves how they could arrive and arise to the calling of being wealthy. It takes grit. It takes smarts. It takes consistency. It takes putting yourself on the line every single day to achieve living like you've never lived before. It may take you being frugal to attain your fortunes. So be it. It may take the sacrifice of giving up the places you love visiting every week or year. So be it.

It may take you being unseen for months and years on end so that you can see your wealth come to reality. Oh well, so be it! Send out your holiday cards early, 'cause you won't be flying around like you used to be.

Stamina

Being that we are working for the long-term goal and success, we must build our stamina daily. With our minds, methods, and emotional behavior, we have to be just like a person training to run the marathon. Stamina is the ability to sustain prolonged physical or mental effort. When it comes to our finances and the creation of wealth, it will take much mental effort. If you think that the journey will be easy, you have another thing coming for you. Here are some tips for building and sustaining your mental effort during the process of building your wealth.

1. Challenge Yourself Constantly

Never settle for where you think your capabilities are for doing something. Always push the envelope. Take a financial course if you've never taken one. Spend an extra hour learning about the stock market. Get your real estate licenses. Do a little more than you are used to each day/week/month. You will be surprised where you end up.

2. Change Up Your Routine

We can get a bit bored after doing the same thing for a very long time. Switch up the routine when this begins to happen. Spice up how you are studying. Dress up when you go to the bank rather than wearing your normal baseball cap and shorts. Find a rooftop to do your daily wealth creation review. Always add a little flavor to your routine. When you do this, it will spark ways of staying interested and motivated to achieve your overall goal for the long term.

3. Rest and Manage Any Stress That Rises Up

We all have to rest at some point. Whether it's getting to bed early, adding meditation to your lifestyle, or listening to classical music (that's one of my methods), make sure you rest, because when we get burned out mentally, everything shuts down. We become lazy, and our attention and focus is at its weakest.

4. Plan for the Slip-Ups and Setbacks

There will be mistakes and wrong decisions made throughout the process, so plan accordingly so that you know what to do if the inevitable (whatever that will be) tends to happen. We all focus on the things that are going well in our lives and can sometimes forget that we can't control the future and the crap that will eventually hit us in the face. Those who plan for the long run tend to plan for the "fast lane moments" and the "pull over, the car is smoking" moments.

5. Visualize the Small and Large Achievements

Keep the goal in mind, always. No matter how long it will take to achieve it. You are on the journey of becoming financially wealthy and, in hindsight, spiritually free and aligned. We constantly tell ourselves to sit tight and stay focused by revisiting the goals we set. It is a true testament that clarity is key. See the goals in the details—the short-term ones, which will lead you to the big one, which will tell the story of how you overcame.

6. Think Positively

No matter what, think positively. The battle will always be of the mind. All things are planned out and orchestrated there, so keep it clear at all times. Anything that will have you thinking of anything other than positive results should be slayed right at the beginning. You have a big goal to achieve, and your mind is what needs to be protected at all times.

Learning Three Steps from Shetty

When we are playing for the long-term reward, it is the process that will always need the most attention and focus. During my time researching and studying, I stumbled upon Jay Shetty, a former monk, who became a huge influencer on and offline, sharing much of his insight and wisdom to the masses around the world. During an interview on a platform called Impact Theory, I spent much time listening, creating notes, and putting what I learned into action. I must say that it has been a big help at times when I continuously go back to the three areas or steps that he specified during his intimate talk. I thought it would be great to align this with having you focus on the long-term goals/rewards. We can't get there without constant evaluation and development of ourselves, which will make our stamina out of this world!

Jay Shetty's Three Steps

1. Observing
2. Shadowing
3. Decision

Observing

While Shetty was talking about the Three Steps, he said that we must open ourselves up to new role

models and new experiences. We must expose ourselves to this continuously. We can't be what we can't
see. How can we be a monk, or a person who is financially stable, or someone who has found peace from
within if we've never seen anyone like that or who has
that type of lifestyle?

Shadowing

Find the role models you are passionate about and
take them seriously. When Shetty was talking about
role models, it didn't have to be specifically a person
but rather a model that has been created that you can
master and be as effective at as the individuals that are
using it. Shadow them, network with them, spend time
with them, and observe them (even from afar). We have
to be addicted to observing that process and lifestyle.
Not the person, but the actual process and lifestyle.

Decision

Make a yes-or-no decision to see if the role model or
lifestyle works for you. Don't focus on the results, just
the hard work that goes with them. You want the most
effective process, not the results. During this step, the
greatest power is self-control, just as a monk's is. This
is exactly as true when we talk about our finances. Self-
control and being level-headed is the key to growth and

financial prosperity. Guess that also goes for our daily development.

Train and Detach the Mind

Shetty stated that we must train our mind and energy to go exactly where we want them to, and when. We have to completely detach and be undeterred from external ups and downs, able to navigate anything (good, bad, happy, sad, excited, angry) with balance.

> **We must not be too excited in pleasure, nor too down in pain.**

We need to be clear-minded and focus on self-purification. A clear head equals clarity in vision, which helps us get what we desire. We must also have good hearts, which in turn lets others know something more about who we are beyond the visions we set before ourselves to achieve. Shetty stated that your passion is for you (this makes you happy), but your purpose is for others (this makes others happy). These all align with each other for the long-term results and constant enjoyment of being on the journey.

Invisible Beliefs

I enjoyed how Shetty was right on point about the belief systems we tend to keep ourselves in. They play a huge role in our walk through life. He stated that invisible beliefs are the things that control our lives, and most of the time we don't even realize it. And if we want these invisible beliefs to stop negatively influencing us, we have to figure out what they are first.

Along with this, he went on to say that one of the most important decisions a person will make in their life is whether they will live in a friendly or hostile universe. Knowing this will help determine if you will be able to achieve what you set out to do over the long term. Hostility can destroy stamina and leave us stagnant. But a friendly universe can allow us to grow, learn, and thrive like we've never done before.

> *"While on the road to long-term results*
> *and rewards, remember that the most successful*
> *individuals are healthy, wealthy, and wise."*
>
> —JAY SHETTY

The Six
Carter Points

14

I was introduced to the music and mindset of Shawn "Jay-Z" Carter when I was thirteen years old. That year, he released his first album, Reasonable Doubt. As a very young entrepreneur, I was tuned in to the business insight he spread throughout each song. As the years came and went, I paid more attention to the verses, interviews, and magazine articles with greater maturity. Being from the poverty-stricken areas and project buildings within my hometown, I felt that he spoke for young men like myself who were just trying to find their way out with their gift from within.

Fast forward to decades later, and I have leveraged many of those wise words he laid down on the albums that we've grown to love. During my initial studying of wealth, I wrote down a collection of six points he made that I felt were important to list as reminders to myself during my journey along this process.

So here are the six points that I hope will push and remind you to stay focused, because if you don't know the famous Jay line, let me remind you: *"I rather die enormous than live dormant. That's how we on it."*

THE SIX
CARTER POINTS

- 1 -

BE YOUR OWN BIGGEST FAN

Believe in whatever you are doing. If
you don't, no one else will.

- 2 -

TAKE CONTROL, THEN LET GO

Work hard and apply yourself in a way that
when the job is done you can look back and
say you have exhausted all possibilities.

- 3 -

FOCUS ON THE PROCESS, NOT THE RESULT

People get consumed by the trappings
of success. They forget the reason why they
do what they do. Keep yourself inspired.

- 4 -

NEVER ACT ON YOUR FEARS

Play the cards, not the money.
You determine your outcome.
Don't make decisions based on fear.

- 5 -

USE MONEY THE RIGHT WAY

Money can be a burden and lead to
bad decisions. But money should make you
comfortable so that you don't compromise
yourself or do anything just for its sake.
Money should give you the freedom
to do what you love.

- 6 -

DON'T STOP GROWING

Growth doesn't stop when you've
become successful.
That's when it starts.

. . . celebrate the hard
work you have done to be truly
aligned on the right path.

The 25
RahGor Proverbs

15

These short RahGor proverbs that you will be reading have been inspired by the Book of Proverbs written by King Solomon. Every single morning, to start my day, I will read a stack of index cards on which I have handwritten various proverbs to remind me of how I should walk and show up in the world as a strong, dynamic, and transparent man of wealth. Each proverb and added insight should be shared among your circle or give you some sense of understanding of how to check yourself and your circle when things are out of line. But it should also be a guide to letting you know that you are taking the right steps and should celebrate the hard work you have done to be truly aligned on the right path.

Wisdom
will keep you away from the wrong people and false words.

Be aware that those who fail to follow the advice of those who came before will always fall into the trap of those who could care less about our goals and dreams of being financially and spiritually free. Wisdom will remind you to research every person you go into business with, pray with, and walk along your journey with. Be wise, and remember the lesson from past experiences and the experiences of others who dealt with people who did harm to others. Don't be too excited by the words of someone you may know nothing about. Anyone can make false financial promises, and toxic hidden agendas that can hurt you to the core sound good. Be wise, and appreciate the wisdom you have received along the way. It will save you continuously.

Follow
the ways of great men with integrity, whose paths are righteous.

E very person alive or has passed away is a blue-print that you can choose to follow. No matter the many blueprints you come to know, just note that those of good character, heart, and spirit will always be the best to follow. They will lead you to lands of milk and honey. Righteous means morally right or justifiable and virtuous. If you intentionally aim to be this way (and follow those who are), you will always show and have integrity in all you do. This in itself is how you remain free and wealthy. If your decisions and actions are made with integrity, you will forever preserve your wealth in all that it's described to be. Seek not to cheat others, because you will end up cheating yourself. Seek not to follow the ill will of ungodly men. Seek to follow the steps of good men who will show you how to illuminate your light.

Respect
and be conscious always
of the higher power.

Be wise in your dealings with all things around you. Never forget that there is a higher power that governs all things. This higher power is also what has created you. So be loyal to that which has created you. That power is God. Be kind in all your dealings, even when you have to show force at times. Whether you are in your boardroom, classroom, or living room, reputation takes years to grow, but only a moment to tarnish. So be of a trusting spirit with the responsibilities that God has given you. Your wealth lies in all that you currently have. Treat all of it as expensive gifts given to you by God, because that is exactly what it is. Expensive blessings. Treat everyone the same way God treats you. And that's with love. Then, you will be able to see all that you no longer have to seek.

Treat everything
you receive as the honoring of
something greater than you.

W hether you are accumulating wealth or currently have it, take care of it the same way you would take care of God's love. This goes for everything that you have the privilege of creating on this beautiful planet. Honor the higher power with your children, friends, money, businesses, careers, and all that you were able to create and attain. You can't receive more if you can't take care of what you have right now. If you appreciate all that you have with care, understanding, attention, and thoughtfulness, God will bless you beyond what your mind can imagine.

You cannot give the best part of your life (another form of wealth) to just anyone or anything. It should be given to God in the form of appreciation, love, humbleness, and faithfulness. Don't lose sight of what and who got you in the position of wealth when all is well. That's not honor, and it's not intelligent. Keep that same energy and faithfulness that you held when you didn't have. If you honor God, he will always bring forth what is good and great for you.

Embrace
wisdom like you were embracing the tree of long life.

Our lives can only be as long lasting as the wisdom we hold on to. We find happiness in the moments we make the right decision by first reflecting on the wisdom bestowed upon us. In all you do, please hold on to the advice of those who gained understanding. We should always be open to receiving all the seeds that can help us to achieve our happiness. Seek to have a firm grip on the wise words that can purify and preserve your life in the years to come.

Don't wait
until tomorrow to help those
who you are able to today.

Help whenever you can. Once you are able to fulfill your needs, everything else is considered overflow. Be sure to direct that overflow to those whose needs aren't met at a specific time. We all fall on hard times, and it would be truly hard to watch those we know tell us they can't help or support us during our time of need, but then splurge right in front of us. So remember to do unto others as you would want others to do unto you.

There is
no rest when you must clear a mess.
And where there is laziness in work ethic,
poverty shall be the boss of the land.

B uilding wealth doesn't take just average actions and thoughts. You must be radical and unconventional in your daily methods. Poverty isn't a place to be or feel comfortable in. You must push wholeheartedly upward and forward. Yes, there will be moments of no rest and sleep. But whatever it will take to be free from the bondage of poverty, so be it. Your life is supposed to be of abundance. To be lazy is to not be abundant. To constantly sleep is to constantly be in poverty. Be not of the spirit of laziness. Be of productivity and abundance, from alpha to omega.

Correct
the wise, and you shall be loved.
Provide insight to the wicked,
and you shall be hated.

Not everyone will appreciate your knowledge or wisdom, so be careful whom you try to bestow it upon. Those who you meet along your path might not always be of good and positive intention. Those who are comfortable being ignorant will never see the light you are providing in their darkness. It is best to deal with those who gravitate to your knowledge of a subject matter. It is best to know that those who are knowledgeable and students of life will always be open to learn from all those who come across their path with no judgment. When you experience being insulted or hurt when you had the best intention in mind, embrace it and move on. There is wealth in understanding that the wise will always appreciate when someone can correct them to have a long-lasting life. Those of the wicked shall never increase in life, for they will never be open to your information, insight, or intelligence.

Anything
gained with tainted
intentions shall be of no true value.

Nothing that is attained by negative force or wrongful ways shall last for very long. It is best to create, build, and attract wealth in the most positive ways possible. Long-lasting headaches and harm come to those who accumulated wealth in the most ignorant, selfish, and shameful ways. It is best to do right and live right while creating your wealth. It may take longer, and it may seem like things aren't clicking together gracefully at times, but trust, when it does, you will have peace of mind, a happy heart, and long well-being.

Wisdom will

allow you to benefit in all your days if you appreciate her. Treat her as less than royalty, and she will make all of your days be of suffering. Your years can be shortened or lengthened depending upon how you value her in your life.

L isten and learn from the ways of the wise. Learn from your past and current mistakes. Learn from your past and current successes. Retain the wisdom from each step you have taken as well as the steps that others have taken. We make sound decisions when we are still and recognize what we know from our previous dealings in the world. We can move mountains and part seas when we make the proper decisions for our lives based upon the insights we know and have applied. If we push insight and wisdom to the side, we will not have anything to protect us, and we will be the ones doing the self-infliction of pain and suffering. And we will be the ones who will break the promises that were once upon our lives.

Wealth
achieved can be a fortress of protection or the beginning of your demise.

S o this is two-fold. To have wealth is to have pro-
tection from poverty. It is the safety net that
we all yearn to have as we grow into adulthood with
major responsibility. The poverty in which many live
is disastrous to their individual lives. It is best to focus
on having a fortress to protect you from the things that
will bring you to ruin.

Now, the other side to this is the following: Wealth
may be a fortress for you, but if you do nothing with
your wealth to battle the systems that keep others in
poverty, then at some point, you will lose wealth in
many ways. This can be in terms of your integrity,
reputation, community, relationships, or peaceful
lifestyle. You cannot attain wealth and not be a lending hand to those in need. Lending doesn't necessarily
mean borrowing money. It could be your knowledge
and resources that allow an individual to climb out of
their bondage independently.

Accept discipline,
and you shall live life with correction and in prosperity.

B e and stay disciplined in all that you do. This road to wealth and freedom isn't one for the weak. It is not one for those with a coward's spirit. You must always be in alignment with the overall vision. Do not fall astray by accepting mediocre invitations to functions that will deplete your resources and tools. Ignore the signs and warnings, and you will be lost. You will waste more time trying to get back on track rather than moving faster on the aligned path to wealth and freedom.

Too much
talk will lead you down
the road to poverty. It will have many
unknown people block opportunities
that were considered for you.

M ove quietly and humbly during your processes of transformation and higher achievement. Speak not of the things you are trying to accomplish all at once. You open the door to criticism and speculation, which will have you at times constantly defending your actions and dreams. Along with this, you must be mindful that not everything you know should be shared. Our mouths can put us in situations that we really didn't want to be in. That's why it's best to think twice, but speak once. So, rest your tongue and allow your actions to speak for you.

It is
a disgrace to be prideful.
Seek humility, and wisdom
shall follow.

Seek to be humble in more ways than one. Our pride can hinder us from growing and can give authority to our egos. This must not happen while on this journey of wealth creation. To have balance is to find patience, understanding, and openness to learn from things greater than where you are. When you connect with others as you move forward, be of kindness and understanding. Do not be of a prideful spirit that will have others be ashamed of you for your ignorance, selfishness, pridefulness, and blindness to the fact that it isn't about you. Know that you are part of a picture greater than your own. And it's important that you not allow your pride to be the color that others wish wasn't in the color pallet.

Honesty
guides many; dishonesty will destroy everything.

B e truthful with every step you take. When you do this, all that comes to you will be for you. What good is it to falsify your way of being and lose all that you attain as soon as you show your true face? It's best to be honest and trustworthy from the beginning. It will guide you to blessings that no person can take from you. If you choose to be dishonest, you will have to deal with the dark consequences of your actions.

Honesty will keep you out of harm's way and will be the sword that slaughters the evil ways of any person who doesn't want to see you achieve your goals. Move with strength and honesty. Let not the dishonesty of anyone hinder you on the path. All things that are true will always come to the light. Be of an honest heart and a truthful tongue.

Be
not the farmer who waits for perfect weather and yet never plants.

Never believe that you should wait for the perfect time to begin creating your wealth, working on your goals, dreaming, or making the change you've always wanted to make. The perfect time will always be right now. If you wait for someone to tell you to go or to endorse your actions, you will miss all the blessings that were created specifically for you. Don't wait, and don't hesitate. Those who do will always be stuck in a stage of potential, never knowing what their lives could actually be. So move on what your heart desires right now. Make the calls, emails, and appointments to plant your seeds. And watch the beautiful things sprout beyond your wildest dreams.

Give

freely and you shall
receive more to give; be generous
and you shall prosper abundantly.

iving should always be part of your plans and lifestyle. Never hold back from serving others in the highest capacity that you know. Hoarding your time, knowledge, resources, connections, and finances doesn't do anything for the environment around you except stagnate it. Those who are wealthy in spirit will always make and find time to give. Those of a poverty-stricken mind will never see the value of helping, giving, and serving. Those who give will prosper continuously, because they make room to receive more. And the more you receive, the more you can give.

Better
to have no spotlight
with a servant than to have a servant
who has no food to serve.

There is no need to be boastful about yourself if you are doing what is right in the shining light. Don't feed into your ego and assume that boasting about having it all is acceptable when you are truly starving. What is extraordinary to one man is normal in the life of another. So trying to be like another person's normal life when it's your extraordinary is destructive. Be humble with your wealth, and don't think or try to be better than someone else. That will only lead you to poverty and toxic environments.

Working
your land brings abundance, but chasing fantasies causes folly.

W orking your land comes in the form of various things such as your job position, business, family, and anything that was given to you by God. You must appreciate and honor God's giving hand by taking care of that which was given to you. Your land has all the food you need to survive every day. If you don't tend to it, your seed will not sprout, and you will have more droughts than you ever had before. Love your land and grow your land as if it is the highest form of telling God, "Thank you."

The second part of this proverb is just as important. Fantasies are false; not real. They are created in the minds of many with very few to no positive results when they've chased them. It makes no sense to take your eyes off the land to chase what never can be. Yes, it's important to dream (and I'm all for achieving big dreams) but not fantasies that are chased with no understanding of the path, the sacrifices that have to be made, and the honest work ethic you must possess to achieve the "unachievable".

There are
benefits to speaking wise words, and rewards for working hard.

S haring the insight and receiving insight for a better way of doing anything is a wealthy benefit. When we receive wise words, it is equivalent to receiving the only winning lottery ticket. And giving wise words just as valuable as giving someone a diamond ring. Wise words give direction, understanding, and guidance for those who need it now or in the future. Wise words show that you or someone has matured from a previous situation. They also show that someone cares enough to shed light on a path that you may be walking in the dark.

Hard work never goes unrewarded. It shows the discipline, grit, and power a person possesses. Hard work is birthed out of a belief system with high standards. Allow hard work to be the negotiator at the table, because actions speak louder than words.

Lies
will always get exposed
when truth is near.

B e honest in all you do so that the credibility of your work will never be erased. Be not of a lying tongue, or all your hard work that you actually did will be in vain.

Don't
be foolish and
show off your knowledge.

B e sure to handle all valuable information and data with care. Make sure that when you present whatever information it may be, it's presented with and received with respect. Showboating what you know doesn't make you or your information more credible. It just makes you look foolish in hopes of gaining ego-driven attention.

Be wise
and walk among the wise. See not to be taught by fools.

Y our circle should always be of wise counsel. The moment that you place yourself around those who lack knowledge or have no thirst for being and wanting more, you will have to live with an empty well that can't replenish you or others who depend upon you.

Lack
of discipline is the
abundance of poverty.

S eek not the wealth all things material. Seek to master your disciplines that allow you to attain wealth in all facets. All too often, we are reminded that the process is the most valuable commodity. It is where we master time, relationship building, and getting a true sense of self. When your discipline is of excellence, your wealth will be of abundance.

Be wise,
and leave behind
proper tools and blueprints for
continuous expansion.

W e won't live forever, but it is important that we are conscious enough to know that we have a younger generation behind us that will need our knowledge and tools we accumulated over the years. This is why it is imperative that we teach the next generation among us how to maintain what is here and how to expand it when we are gone. This also goes for our children and their children's children. All the wealth we accumulate should be preserved (invested) properly so that there isn't a lack of tools to keep things going and growing. This is what the wise do with no hesitation.

Be careful
of all insight received.
Question everything twice.

N o information of importance comes as easy as a gentle breeze, at least not most of the time. Truth is usually scattered, and you will come to recognize that most people will claim to have it. Question all messengers of knowledge and insight. Never go into any situation believing everything you read, see, and hear. Collect all pieces of information, and make a profound conclusion. This, my friend, is wisdom.

Seek
patience for
full understanding.

Anything of supreme value is never rushed. Whether we are talking about opulence or excellence, its path is patience. It's best to pray for patience, because you will be tested constantly throughout your process. Even when you finally understand a step that took you repeated tries to make, you will unfortunately have to do it all over again moving forward. But if you have patience, you will be knowledgeable and wise in understanding what it takes to achieve the unachievable.

Poems

These are

the poems that keep me focused

during my process of creating wealth . . .

~

If

By Rudyard Kipling

If you can keep your head when all about you
  Are losing theirs and blaming it on you;
If you can trust yourself when all men doubt you,
  But make allowance for their doubting too:
If you can wait and not be tired by waiting,
  Or, being lied about, don't deal in lies,
Or being hated don't give way to hating,
  And yet don't look too good, nor talk too wise;

If you can dream—and not make dreams your master;
  If you can think—and not make thoughts your aim,
If you can meet with Triumph and Disaster
  And treat those two impostors just the same:
If you can bear to hear the truth you've spoken
  Twisted by knaves to make a trap for fools,
Or watch the things you gave your life to, broken,
  And stoop and build'em up with worn-out tools;

If you can make one heap of all your winnings
  And risk it on one turn of pitch-and-toss,
And lose, and start again at your beginnings,

And never breathe a word about your loss:
If you can force your heart and nerve and sinew
   To serve your turn long after they are gone,
   And so hold on when there is nothing in you
Except the Will which says to them: "Hold on!"

If you can talk with crowds and keep your virtue,
Or walk with Kings—nor lose the common touch,
   If neither foes nor loving friends can hurt you,
   If all men count with you, but none too much:
      If you can fill the unforgiving minute
      With sixty seconds' worth of distance run,
   Yours is the Earth and everything that's in it,
   And—which is more—you'll be a Man, my son!

Don't Quit

BY EDGAR A. GUEST

When Things go wrong, as they sometimes will,
When the road you're trudging seems all uphill,
When the funds are low and debts are high,
And you want to smile but have to sigh.
When care is pressing you down a bit,
Rest, if you must, but don't you quit.

Life is queer with its twists and turns,
As everyone of us sometimes learns,
And many a failure turns about,
When he might have won if he'd stuck it out,
Don't give up though the pace seems slow,
You might succeed with another blow.

Often the struggler has given up,
When he might captured the victor's cup.
And he learned too late, when the night slipped down,
How close he was to the golden crown,

Success is failure turned inside out,
The silver tint of clouds of doubt,
And you never can tell how close you are,
It may be near when it seems afar,
So stick to the fight when you're hardest hit,
It's when things seem worst that you mustn't quit.

How Did You Die?

BY EDMUND VANCE COOKE

Did you tackle that trouble that came your way
With a resolute heart and cheerful?
Or hide your face from the light of day
With a craven soul and fearful?
Oh, a trouble's a ton, or a trouble's an ounce,
Or a trouble is what you make it,
And it isn't the fact that you're hurt that counts,
But only how did you take it?

You are beaten to earth? Well, well, what's that?
Come up with a smiling face.
It's nothing against you to fall down flat,
But to lie there—that's disgrace.
The harder you're thrown, why the higher you
bounce;
Be proud of your blackened eye!
It isn't the fact that you're licked that counts,
It's how did you fight—and why?

And though you be done to the death, what then?
If you battled the best you could,
If you played your part in the world of men,
Why, the Critic will call it good.
Death comes with a crawl, or comes with a pounce,
And whether he's slow or spry,
It isn't the fact that you're dead that counts,
But only how did you die?

Good Timber

By Douglas Malloch

The tree that never had to fight
For sun and sky and air and light,
But stood out in the open plain
And always got its share of rain,
Never became a forest king
But lived and died a scrubby thing.

The man who never had to toil
To gain and farm his patch of soil,
Who never had to win his share
Of sun and sky and light and air,
Never became a manly man
But lived and died as he began.

Good timber does not grow with ease:
The stronger wind, the stronger trees;
The further sky, the greater length;
The more the storm, the more the strength.
By sun and cold, by rain and snow,
In trees and men good timbers grow.

Where thickest lies the forest growth,
We find the patriarchs of both.
And they hold counsel with the stars
Whose broken branches show the scars
Of many winds and much of strife.
This is the common law of life.

On Quitting

BY EDGAR ALBERT GUEST

How much grit do you think you've got?
Can you quit a thing that you like a lot?
You may talk of pluck; it's an easy word,
And where'er you go it is often heard;
But can you tell to a jot or guess
Just how much courage you now possess?

You may stand to trouble and keep your grin,
But have you tackled self-discipline?
Have you ever issued commands to you
To quit the things that you like to do,
And then, when tempted and sorely swayed,
Those rigid orders have you obeyed?

Don't boast of your grit till you've tried it out,
Nor prate to men of your courage stout,
For it's easy enough to retain a grin
In the face of a fight there's a chance to win,
But the sort of grit that is good to own
Is the stuff you need when you're all alone.

How much grit do you think you've got?
Can you turn from joys that you like a lot?
Have you ever tested yourself to know
How far with yourself your will can go?
If you want to know if you have grit,
Just pick out a joy that you like, and quit.

It's bully sport and it's open fight;
It will keep you busy both day and night;
For the toughest kind of a game you'll find
Is to make your body obey your mind.
And you never will know what is meant by grit
Unless there's something you've tried to quit.

About the Author

R AHFEAL "RAHGOR" GORDON is recognized as one of the top international orators and leadership advisors for world leaders and global entrepreneurs who seek to effectively impact the global community through business, education, and politics. For over a decade, RahGor has been leveraging the core fundamentals that promote productivity and success. His lectures, keynote speeches, workshops, and books provide in-depth strategies in the areas of personal development, global leadership, and entrepreneurship to those aiming to achieve success. RahGor's key insight into culture development for business and organizational leaders makes his impact on an individual's personal and business performance highly effective.

RahGor has written and published a total of 17 books combined. He is the principal owner of **Madison + Park**, a full-service global branding and publishing agency that assists entrepreneurs, corporations, and global influencers with becoming leaders in their industry. He became the global mentor and advisor for **The Queen's Young Leaders Program**, a program in the United Kingdom that was established by the Queen Elizabeth Diamond Jubilee Trust in honor of Her Majesty Queen Elizabeth II of the United Kingdom lifetime of service to the Commonwealth.

He is the Global Ambassador of the **International Hub** in Oslo, Norway, which houses and provides resources for start-up entrepreneurs from 21 different countries. RahGor also co-founded the **Voices for World Peace Organization**, a platform that brings together a diverse group of global leaders and youth to work in solidarity to eradicate issues such as extremism, terrorism, and inequality by sharing ideas and creating strategies to bring peace and unity to areas of conflict around the world.